Looking for LYRICS

The Song In My Heart

Edited by Donna Samworth

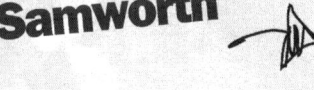

First published in Great Britain in 2009 by:

Young Writers
Remus House
Coltsfoot Drive
Peterborough
PE2 9JX
Telephone: 01733 890066
Website: www.youngwriters.co.uk

All Rights Reserved
Book Design by Spencer Hart & Tim Christian
© Copyright Contributors 2009
SB ISBN 978-1-84924-700-9

Foreword

Young Writers was established in 1991 to nurture creativity in our children and young adults, to give them an interest in poetry and an outlet to express themselves. Seeing their work in print will encourage them to keep writing as they grow, and become our poets of tomorrow.

Selecting the poems has been challenging and immensely rewarding. The effort and imagination invested by these young writers makes their poems a pleasure to enjoy reading time and time again.

Contents

Shormee Aziz (14)	1
Lisa Manning (16)	2
Lauren Finlay (15)	4
Alysha Lauren Davies (14)	5
Reannah Brooks (12)	6
Laura Wynne (15)	7
Gerard Loughran (22)	8
Christopher Young (17)	9
Bryony Porter-Collard (15)	10
Georgina Salzedo (14)	11
Nicola McCaig (13)	12
Catherine Peach (15)	13
Corie Graham Pritchard (16)	14
Hannah King (13)	15
Sophie Louise Elizabeth Prendiville-Fox (15)	16
Danielle Mitchell (15)	17
Georgina Emery (15)	18
Kerry Anne Wells (16)	19
Isaac Lister (14)	20
Dannielle Pearce (14)	21
Tessa Mann (15)	22
Lucy House (17)	23
Hetti Sansom (19)	24
Shona Jackson (15)	25
Helen Monks (16)	26
Jess Rushworth (15)	27
Sophie Curran (14)	29
Sophie Kelly (15)	29
Robyn-Marie Kenyon (13)	30
Shilpa Sisodia (15)	31
Jordaine Henningham (15)	32
Vicki Good (14)	33
Scott McCutcheon (16)	34
Dale Manning (16)	35
Tom Nixon (15)	36
Eleanor Gregory (13)	37
Jack Fenton (15)	38
Hazel Gambles (13)	39
Michela Scarpa & Lauren Santana (17)	40
Amy Louise Jones (15)	41
Kirsty Johnston (19)	42
Cameron Donaghy (11) & Ashley Donaghy (13)	43
Natalie Dickinson (13)	44
Nicole Leigh Topham (15)	45
Katy Brown (15)	46
Nicole Robinson (14)	47
Daniel Keith	48
Emily Whittingham (15)	49
Tiffany Ching (15)	50
Aaron Parr (15)	51
Kiera Whitbread	52
Bethany Foley (17)	53
Jessica Frost (14)	54
Hannah Mereweather (13)	55
Jennifer Downing (13)	56
Lauren Hay (14)	57
Katiey Alice Vine (14)	58
Michelle Neal (16)	59
Matthew Davenport & Robert Bond (12)	60
Helena Clough (15)	61
Jennifer Glover (15)	62
Simon Ball (14)	63
Holly Thwaites-Bee (16)	64
Joanna Henshall (14)	65
Sarah Hughes (16)	66
Amy Cooper (13)	67
Demi Peters (15)	68
Katie Burton (13)	69
Hayley Wragg (16)	70
Anfernee Duncombe (13)	71
Amy Wootton	72
India Collen (13)	73
Amie Shave (11)	74
Victory Sanu-Goodness (13)	75
Bethany O'Shea (12)	76
Ellie Rice (13)	77
Jonathan Young (16)	78
Tyler-Megan Barnett (12)	79
Jessica Deacon (12)	80

Chelsea Turner (13) 81	Tahja Ronai Adeyingbo (12) 123
Victoria Ankin (14) 82	Susan Dowell (14) 124
Rose Grounds (16) 83	Chloe Mason (13) 125
Leah Watts (14) 84	Charlotte Simpson (13) 125
Faye McCue (12) 85	Charlotte Baldwin (13) 126
Paul Constable (14) 86	Jack Radford (14) 126
Rebecca Grant (15) 87	Toni Solly (12) 127
Jessica Elderfield (14) 88	Emily Mills (14) 128
Miles Staplehurst (13) 89	Tom Sandry (16) 129
Phoebe White (13) 90	Holly Blood (14) 130
Charlie Shute (14) 91	Zoe Hunt (16) 131
Stephanie Louise Heyes (14) 92	Katy Dell (14) 132
Anne O'Neill (12) 93	Benjamin Cope (17) 133
Courtney Jayne Duckworth (14) 94	Sebastien Reece (10) 134
Kieran Vyas (17) 95	Amy O'Meara (12) 135
Arnold McCullough (13) 96	Dannielle Rose (13) 136
Daniel Roberts (14) 97	Alanna Holdsworth (15) 137
Rachel Stirr (12) 98	Olivia Church (13) 138
Caitlin Sweeney (12) 99	Kayleigh Tompkins (14) 139
Holly May Dixon (16) 100	Jezel Jones (17) 140
Lauren Kerbyson (17) 100	Reann Radcliffe (15) 141
Michelle Murei (16) 101	Heather King (15) 142
Jade Gullidge (11) 101	Taeeba Rahim (9) 143
David Rees (14) 102	Katie Whelpton (14) 143
Ashley Donaghy (13) 102	Hannah Garrett (13) 144
Charlotte Murray (14) 103	Stephen Shelmerdine (15) 145
Jessica Jarvis (13) 104	Eleanor Hynds (14) 146
Matt McKay (19) 105	Melissa Gardner (16) 147
Haya Mulhem (12) 106	Kellie Williams (14) 148
Jade Tomlins (15) 107	Charlotte Elizabeth West (10) 148
Rebecca Wyatt (14) 108	Alexandra Pointer (19) 149
Caris Twyman (12) 109	Bethany Picton (12) 150
Rebecca Ingram-Jones (15) 110	Alice Langridge (14) 151
Mishelle Waqasi (15) 111	Ella Stirling (15) 152
Lydia McCarthy (13) 112	Jasmine Blanchard (12) 153
Nisha Ahmed (14) 113	Hannah Clarke (13) 153
Paige Lauren Izquierdo (12) 114	Olivia Faith Emmerson (12)
Shelby Lucier (12) 115	& Arlo Emmerson-Hewitt (7) 154
Harriette Cooke (15) 116	Chloe Mulholland (11) 154
Rebecca Booth (15) 117	Cathy Ross (16) 155
Nathan Harrop (12) 118	Rosalind Bruce (18) 156
Holly Taylor (13) 119	Kirsten Mace (14) 157
Jasmine Bayes (14) 120	Anneka Honeyball (14) 158
Rosemary Cowhig (17) 121	Holly Riordan (13) 159
Jessica Perks (14) 122	Caitlin Kinney (13) 159

Name	Page
Lauren Wilkes (13)	160
Zoë Powell (13)	161
Lily Potter (10)	162
Bethany Chipperfield (13)	163
James Williams (16)	164
Samantha Smart (13)	165
Megan Parkinson (13)	166
Fleur Bowler (12)	167
Francesca Stoddart (9)	168
Omolara Omoniyi (14)	168
Gabi Martin (15)	169
Abigail Leighton (12)	170
Chris Driscoll (22)	171
Sara Siddiqui (15)	171
Chloe Howard (14)	172
Stephanie Kenna (12)	172
Luisa Raucci (12)	173
Abbie Culf (12)	173
Ryan Lee (14)	174
Alice Cracknell (16)	175
Kiya Burgess (13)	176
Chloe Runkee (13)	177
Eleanor Spawton (14)	178
Jarlath Hagan (16)	178
Kayleigh Patchett (18)	179
Jenna Rainey (16)	179
Sophie Grace White (13)	180
Melanie Rumble (12)	181
Lauren McLaughlin (14)	182
Ceri Davis	183
Emma Henderson (15)	184
Kainaat Mahmood (12)	184
Theresa Locock (15)	185
Sophie Forbes (13)	185
Adelaine Ingram (11)	186
Hannah Russell (10)	186
Kieran Jones (14)	187
Chloé Branagan-Liddy (12)	188
Nana Adwoa Asiedu (18)	189
Chloe Harris (14)	190
Katrina Keatley (13)	191
Emily Ashmore (10)	192
Martha King (12)	193
Elle Reynolds (9)	193
Nathan Adam Walters (12)	194
Adam Freeman (18)	194
Zoe Peterkin (15)	195
Chloe Burrell (12)	196
Darcie Lowrie (12)	197
Jade Haley (14)	198
Kisshanath Alankaratheepan (13)	199
Samantha Bull (14)	200
Ollivia Dale (13)	201
Conner Doidge (14)	201
Laura Samuel (16)	202
Phoebe Corser (15)	202
Brendan Johnson (17)	203
Beatrice Grist-Perkins (14)	204
James Hill (14)	205
Katie Thorne (15)	205
Emma Craddock (17)	206
Kirstie Hember (13)	207
Georgia Kirk (11)	208
Kerrie Arnold (12)	208
Charlie Schofield (14)	209
Sherri Lewis (17)	210
Corrinna Osborne (14)	211
Oliver Redmond (12)	212
Sarah Campbell (14)	213
Nina Prells (15)	214
Francesca Vinall (12)	215
Kerry-Ann Collar (9)	215
Lynsey Ann Petrie (14)	216
Louise Smith (14)	217
Chloe Fitzsimons (15)	218
Joe Hollamby (15)	219
Chanelle Andrews (13)	220
Buki Fatuga (16)	221
Anya Holland (14)	222
Emily Rose Derrick (10)	223
Scott Milne (15)	224
Louisa Sham (16)	225
Kerry Spillane (16)	226
Eleanor Rose Bumby (8)	226
Hannah Taylor (17)	227
Rhys Clarke (16)	227
George Bowman (12)	228
Emily Deborah Webb (16)	229
Tommy Birchall (15)	230
Caitlin O'Riordan (15)	231

Thomas Bayliss (15)	232
Lauren McFarland (13)	233
Ashleigh Pagani (17)	234
Marley Fancourt (16)	235
Hayley Garner (14)	236
Freya Nicholls (14)	237
Rachel Finn (15)	238
Shauna Burgess (13)	239
Aylish Gray (14)	240
Hannah Fox (11)	241
Amanda Hall (16)	242
Lucy Paisley (13)	243
Sarah Russell (13)	244
Hayley Stronge (11)	245
Amber Simpson (13)	246
Abigail Irvin (13) & Marc Irvin (12)	247
Cherish Thorpe (14)	248
Laura Smart (17)	249
Paige Harper (17)	250
Anna Helen Heywood (12)	251
Mia-Sara Crowther-Nicol (17)	252
Rebecca Wilson (15)	253
Stephen Hamilton (16)	254
Madeline Wilding (16)	255
Cody Frowen (14)	256
Aimee May Walker (13)	257
Lucy Robson (13)	258
George Styers (13)	259
Caroline Inker (16)	260
Conor McLean (14)	261
Sam Jellard (15)	262
Hannah Sabin (18)	263
Emma Louise Carter (13)	264
Georgia May Cresswell (10)	264
Catherine O'Neill (14)	265
Millie Clarke (16)	265
Leanne Drain (15)	266
Yasmin Anderson (14)	267
Aaron McBride (18)	268
Billie-Jean Bradley (12)	269
Jessica White (13)	270
Louis Metcalf Salerno (11)	271
Katy Ingoldsby (14)	272
Philip Bosah (17)	273
Alexandra Dunn (16)	274
Thabile Mdhluli (12)	274
Scott Wilson (16)	275
Amy Taggart (14)	275
Danielle Clarke (11)	276
Tariq Bushara (13)	276
Ali Mansfield (15)	277
Kelsey Griffin (15)	277
Amy Clark (14)	278
Cath Nobbs (10)	278
Charlotte Hilsdon (17)	279
Stephanie Henry (16)	279
Madeline King (13)	280
Amy Wooding (16)	280
Nina Baldwin (15)	281
Jack Burton (13)	281
Georgina Wong (13)	282
Aaron James Walton (12)	282
Kirsty Keatch (17)	283
Tarryn Layla Hiller (14)	283
Nicole Andrea Gonzalez (12)	284
Priyashree K Patel (16)	284
Kelly Scutt (16)	285
Stephanie Jane Parker (8)	285
Catriona Mair (13)	286
Erin Harvey (12)	286
Daisy Caig (13)	287
Leah Knox (12)	287
Lisa Fairley (16)	288
Jessica Cordery Prince (13)	288
Catriona Cormack (12)	289
Jasmine Clarke (10)	289
Harry Sadeghi (19)	290
Paige Band (12)	290
Lauren Degenhardt (15)	291
Megan Roberts (14)	291
Jade Bond (12)	292
Michelle Vincent (18)	292
Lucy Jane Wilkinson (13)	293
Claire Harrity (15)	293
David Elliott (15)	294
Caitlin Kitchener (15)	294
Katherine Kennedy (18)	295
André White	295
Anna Goodman-Jones (16)	296

The Poems

Equality

What does it matter of the colour of my skin?
What does it matter my home language that I speak?
What does it matter of my cultural beliefs?
Is that so important that we start war over these little things?

What does it matter whether I'm black or white
Asian or light, yeah what a fright
Does it not matter what lays inside?
Does no one care anymore, as all they do is fight?

And I try to tell them 'bout equality
But they care about whether I'm wrong or right
As they're always judging me about the stupid things
As whether I'm black or white.

Why should it matter the colour of my skin?
I'm done with wishing there was some justice to this.

It seems you people get your kicks from hurting me
Does it not matter on how I feel?
Every day I feel like I'm breaking in
To little pieces. I can't seem to resolve this.

And I try to tell them 'bout equality
But they care about whether I'm wrong or right
As they're always judging me about the stupid things
As whether I'm black or white.

Why should it matter the colour of my skin?
I'm done with wishing there was some justice in this.

I wish for equality, I wish for love
Why can't we all join as one?
I've always been given grief for who I am
Why can't they just accept me for who I am?
Why is it the going always gets so tough
And why is it that my days always seem to be so rough?
And it seems that I have n rights
Always invisible to your sights
Won't anybody help me?

Shormee Aziz (14)

Kiss My Base

Baby, when I need a fix
I just need to turn on the switch
So I hope you really know
That I'm just the best
So please be impressed.

Because you thought you took the wrong girl
Completely ages ago
I hope you'll pay damages
For my unbeating, broken heart.

You say I'm an animal
You know that I know it all
I said that should have gotten lost
Before because you're no good to me
You say that I'm musical
You know that I have it all.

So kiss my base
Kiss my base, kiss my base
If you wanna
Boy, just kiss my base
Kiss my base, kiss my base.

Boy, you say I'm the luckiest
Man
Just to be with a girl, like you
You put hand in your pocket
Just to pull our necklace
But it was for another girl.

I was angry and crying over you
So I went home and never came out for two whole days

You say I'm an animal
You say that I've got all
I said that should have gotten lost before
Because pure no good to me
You say that I'm musical
You know that I have it all

So just kiss my base
Kiss my base, kiss my base

If you wanna
Boy, just kiss my base
Kiss my base, kiss my base
If you wanna

Cos you're no good to me

I said useless, stupid and pathetic
Because it's all you really are
So take your bimbo home
And never ever come back

You say I'm an animal
You say I got it all
I said I should have gotten lost, lost
Before because you're no good to me

So just kiss my base
Kiss my base, kiss my base
If you wanna
Boy, just kiss my base
Kiss my base, kiss my base
If you wanna

So just kiss my base
Kiss my base, kiss my base
If you wanna
Boy, just kiss my base
Kiss my base, kiss my base
If you wanna

I said useless, stupid and pathetic
Because it's all you really are
So take your bimbo home
And never ever come back

Cos you're not the one for me.

Lisa Manning (16)

Ready Or Not

Ooh, just spotted you
Lookin' so fine
I'm wonderin'
Do you have the time
To spend with me?
I'm gonna make you mine
Do you want a little bump and grind?

But I don't know if you can handle me
And my girls gonna be a scandal
Most guys too scared to get with me
Come, show me you got a little superiority.

Boy, you lookin' hot
Let me take you to the candy shop
Wanna rock with you, show me what you got
I'm comin' baby, ready or not
Just give me a chance and I'll make you happy
The game is on, so let's play pappie
I'm feelin' you, so just accept me
I'm comin' baby, ready or not.

Ooh, you caught me
Starin' at you
Boy let me know
Do you feel it too?
Our chemistry undeniable
Come on over here, I'm waitin' for you.

But see I'm a lil' too shy to talk to you
So I need you to make the first move
If you promise you won't hurt me, babe
Take me back to your place and I'll play your slave.

Boy you lookin' hot
Let me take you to the candy shop
Wanna rock with you, show me what you got
I'm comin' baby, ready or not
Just give me a chance and I'll make you happy
The game is on, so let's play pappie
I'm feelin' you so just accept me
I'm comin' baby, ready or not.

Now boy, I've been waitin' for you all night long
And now the DJ's playin' my favourite song
I be breakin' it down, come join me beau
This be how the girls from GNL do it.

Boy you lookin' hot
Let me take you to the candy shop
Wanna rock with you, show me what you got
I'm comin' baby, ready or not
Just give me a chance and I'll make you happy
The game is on, so let's play pappie
I'm feelin' you so just accept me
I'm comin' baby, ready or not.

Boy you lookin' hot
Let me take you to the candy shop
Wanna rock with you, show me what you got
I'm comin' baby, ready or not
Just give me a chance and I'll make you happy
The game is on, so let's play pappie
I'm feelin' you so just accept me
I'm comin' baby, ready or not.

Watch out! Yeah!

Lauren Finlay (15)

Miss You

I miss you,
I miss your smile,
I miss you every time you walk on by,
This tear in my eyes is just to see you smile
Because you know I really can't say goodbye.
You really are the world to me and it's about time your realised,
When my achy heart is on the line 'cause it's hard to say goodbye.
So please just tell me you don't know why
You always wave me goodbye and now all I want to do is cry
Because I miss you more the days go by.

Alysha Lauren Davies (14)

Livin' The Dream

When I was young
I sang along
To every song that came to my ears
I wanted to be famous
I wanted to be a singer
Because I had a dream!

I am a rocker
And I have a dream
To get up on the stage
And hear fans scream
I am a rocker
Taking things easy
Cos I'm living the dream!

I sing on stage
Whilst the audiences rage
I stage-dived
The concert ended
I just thrived.

So now I am a rock star
Living the dream
Bet you wish you were me!

I am a rocker
And I have a dream
To get up on the stage
And hear fans scream
I am a rocker
Taking things easy
Cos I'm living the dream!

When I was young
I sang along
To every song that came to my ears
I wanted to be famous
I wanted to be a singer
Because I had a dream!

I am a rocker
And I have a dream
To get up on the stage
And hear fans scream
I am a rocker
Taking things easy
Cos I'm living the dream!

I sing on stage
Whilst the audiences rage
I stage-dived
The concert ended
I just thrived.

So now I am a rock star
Living the dream
Bet you wish you were me!

I am a rocker
And I have a dream
To get up on the stage
And hear fans scream
I am a rocker
Taking things easy
Cos I'm living the dream!

Reannah Brooks (12)

Run

Every day I wake up with a smile
To think I might get a chance to see your face again
But I can't call you now cos I'm lost in my head
The pressure's rising and I just can't take it
So I'm gonna run, run, run away
From everything that gets in the way
Of what we've got and I will never stop
Until we're safe with the love that we've got.

Laura Wynne (15)

My Mother

I've been trying so long
To write a song, about my mama
It's such an honour, to call her my mama
I apologise, for any of the drama,
That I cause you,
I would be lost, if I ever did lose you,
If life did a re-do, I would always choose you,
No replacement, no erasing,
To my amazement, you is amazing,
When I was hell-raising
You was heaven-gazing,
Turned my bad, to better, and my better
To us together forever,
You the water to my river
The pumps to my heart
The most beautiful type of art
An all these girls in my life,
From girlfriends until I have a wife
You is the one who shines so bright
You the gravity
That holds down everything right
So I thank you forever
I'm crying tears of joy, so I'm crying river
That's my mother and I love her.

Gerard Loughran (22)

Untitled

If once you looked forward
Without looking back
You may break a smile
And drive on with life
For a thousand more miles

Live for the moment
Dance to the movement
Point to the sky
And smile . . .

Arms in the air
Let's create a world banner
Let our message soar
A point worth listening to
That no one can ignore

Live for the moment
Dance to the movement
Point to the sky
And smile . . .

A cure for our problems and needs
Let the airwaves shake
With a sound like no other
Scream if you need to
Our message is uplifting

Live for the moment
Dance to the movement
Point to the sky
And smile . . .

Christopher Young (17)

Lost

What's Your Mum Like?
Well I couldn't tell you if I wanted to
I haven't seen her for over seven years
She died when I was two
I wish I had known her
Known what it was like having a mother
Always being there
Loving me like no other

You see I need a mum
To teach me important life skills
To keep me on the straight and narrow
Instead I'm popping pills
I'm living on the street
Cold and alone
I don't know who I'll meet
Out here on my own

'OK, what about your dad?'
My dad don't make me laugh
He left when I was four
Didn't even say goodbye
Just slammed that door

Didn't feel it then but I'm glad
I didn't need him
He was never a good dad
Always shouting
Being mean
But the worst thing was
He hit me

During the day he was nice
Hugs and talking to me
But come nightfall the drink would change him
He was not who he used to be

So I cried and I screamed
Praying someone would hear
Pleading to be set free
But no one came

'But where do you live?'
I live wherever life takes me
I never stay in one place for long
I guess I'm running from myself
Can't think, got to stay strong

Well, here's my stop
'But wait, will you be OK?'
You look down and then back up
Fatal mistake, I am gone
Gone to end another day

No one knows my full story
No one will ever
Alone, doing nothing right
Be with someone? Never
These are my thoughts as I settle down for the night
Feeling the hard ground, feeling the frost
This is my life; cold, alone and lost.

Bryony Porter-Collard (15)

Two Hearts

You're the ballerina
And I'm the tin soldier
But I didn't manage to die

You had my heart
As the flames engulfed you
But I didn't manage to die

Two hearts died
But one is still beating
Two hearts burned
But one is still in flames
Your heart died
But mine is still bleeding
Your heart burned
And I still feel the pain
Of the flame.

Georgina Salzedo (14)

Wasted Moments

(In memory of my grandad, George Livesey, he never wasted a moment)

There's a rose that sings in summer
And an orchid that flourishes in fall
If the wind won't carry their pollen
Then they won't know to grow big and tall

I saw an angel whisper softly
To another in handsome blue and gold
She whispered, 'Can you hear those trumpets?'
And I said, 'That's your life being sold.'

If we don't savour the moments
Then why have moments at all?
If we don't hang onto the best bits
Then we'll wilt like orchids in fall.

If the shutters close
And the cold moon rise
Then we should be left with tears in our eyes.

There are two people across the street
At separate ends, not likely to meet
But when I saw the chance, I took it soon
And now they're on their honeymoon

If you see a sad little bluebird
Whose feathers aren't quite so blue
Then why don't you go and help him?
You'll both feel good for a while or two.

If we don't savour the moments
Then why have moments at all?
If we don't hang onto the best bits
Then we'll wilt like orchids in fall.

If the shutters close
And the cold moon rise
Then we should be left with tears in our eyes.

As for my life, it's a tale
An adventure or so I'm told
But the truth will out forever
I'll be tellin' my story even when I'm old.

When the shutters closed
And the cold moon rose
I was left there with tears on my nose

I didn't want to savour the moments
In my head they kept spinning round
I didn't want to hang onto the best bits
They fall and burn to the ground.

Nicola McCaig (13)

Lights Out

This is all because of
You and my mind
I only ever dreamed
Of something like this
Didn't think you were real
Then you were saved
And I found you all only.

I don't know what sleep
Is anymore, the lights go out
And I'm laying in my bed
Wishing there was more
To what we have now.

Hoping you're never
Going to change for me
Because I love every part of you
Stay the way you are
You're my everything
And this the way it has to be
You and me together forever.

I don't know what sleep
Is anymore, the lights go out
And I'm laying in my bed
Wishing there was more
To what we have now
This is how it's going to end for me.

Catherine Peach (15)

Sitting In A Box Square Room

Sitting in a box-square room
Just thinkin' about how I hurt you
It makes me want to laugh a bit
You're with her and now I just feel sick
And times have changed and so have we
But tell me how you still love me
Cos life is love and love is all I see
But I will forget, oh, I will forget
Every lie and every vision
All the times electric collision
You demand I pick myself up
Wash my hands and do my make-up
But who's to see?
I'm here out of luck
Nothing more, the lightning's struck, in me
And you won't see my face
Oh, she won't let you see my face
No more, no more, my heart . . . no more
And here's to life
And here's to me
And here's to every bad time retreat. Defeat.
This is how my heart will beat
A thump and pause
I'm incomplete
I think I'm incomplete
Maybe this is good
To learn from your mistakes
But don't forget the words you spoke
Cos I try to say them but I choke
And she just loves to provoke
Me and you, me and you
You and me, you and her

Well, I wish you well, you both look great
I hear her voice and your sweet face
This is it and this is me
Just don't forget to not believe.

Promise me you won't believe.

Corie Graham Pritchard (16)

Dream Catcher

Take my hand
Fly with me
To a place
They'll never see

Take my hand
See my dream
Look with your heart
And you'll believe

Step out the window
Into the night
Let your mind run free
Let your body
Take flight
Feel the magic now
Lift your arms
And love it.

Chorus
Dream catcher
Live your life
Dream catcher
Lift off and fly
Follow yours
I'll follow mine
Let your mind
Reverse the time
Spend half your life dreaming
You can make it come true.

Hannah King (13)

Pops Fox
(RIP-11.09.08)

My Pops Fox and I have a special star
And no matter where we are
I wish I may, I wish I might
We make a wish each and every night
I wish for him to have tomorrow
For our time never to end in sorrow.

Thank you Pops for being you and letting me be me
Sorry, I didn't get to know you as much as all my other cousins
But Frank, my dad, just didn't want to know me
If we were close like him and my little sis
We might have said goodbye and a goodnight kiss
Words could never express how I feel
But thinking of you and Nannie Carmen made my life so very real
I don't know where I would be today
If my lovely mum didn't guide me along the way
What comes next, I do not know
But I will use my life to show
I may not talk, but I can surely think
Mum tells me I am very clever like my Pappy Fox family
(But then she says its Pops you liked)
Then I go quiet and go to ride my bike
People think I am thick because I cannot say things
But the words ring out (and hurt) but they surely stay
But losing you and then my nannie Carmen - RIP (13.09.08)
The pain I just cannot explain
I cannot write, I cannot talk but on my computer
I can surely talk.
I know what to say and understand but the words don't come out
And I am left with pain but I know that you're with my nan, you understand
These are my words that I have written
But I am left here with a big lump in my throat
The hurt and the pain that I am feeling
But my mum is here to help me with dealing
I am sorry Pops, I can't say goodbye

But promise you in my heart you will never die
I'll hold you dearly in my thoughts and heart
For all the years and years we have missed
Goodnight my pops and rest in peace
Please look after my nannie Carmen so my heart's at ease.

Sophie Louise Elizabeth Prendiville-Fox (15)

I'll Just Have To Pretend

I will never be over you
But I'm done with dreaming my time away
You'll never love me, not the way I want
But loving you this much has led my heart astray
My heart still skips a beat whenever I hear your name
It's true, we are all just victims of love
Because love has me playing this heartbreaking game.

Is that all love is?
Just an ache in the heart
I spent so long now trying to make you see
We were never meant to be apart
I've been searching for you, but I guess I was too late
It was always meant for you and me
But I guess I have to face that we're just friends
I could never not love you
So I guess I'll just have to pretend.

I've spent so long hoping you'll finally see
I've watched you be happy with someone else
I accept that me and you were never meant to be
But you'll never know that you were the one
You'll never know how much time I lost waiting for you
I have to face the truth . . .
But through it all I wouldn't have it any other way
My feelings for him I will never show
Maybe I'll find the courage to tell him some day
For now I'm OK for him to never know.

Danielle Mitchell (15)

Untitled

I don't remember how we got to this place
But I had your scent lingering on my skin
We were chasing lights to make the moment last
As if we could put off forever by just another day
We're trapped here in this subconscious state
Where nothing moves and yet we can't keep up

Blinded by the dark
Swallowed by the soulless
Pin me down, bind me tight
Not a lot can cure this

Everything about this makes me want to disappear
It's not quite a nightmare but it isn't a dream
I feel no pulse but I'm still alive
And soaking my spine is bitter fear
That you won't be there once I've walked this line and
That the sky will fall in and the stars will be gone

Enlightened by the glow
Washed up by the wanting
Let me go, untie me here
I think I know the solution

I read the lines etched on your skin
Why are you showing me this now?
It's far too late for such things
I heard the words you spoke to me
You don't need to say this now
There's no need for you to do this

Tell me whose
Whose
Whose
Tell me whose side are you on
The good or the better?

Tell me how
How
How
Tell me how you became who you
Seem to think you are?

Brightened by the glare
Refreshed by the honest
I'm free, no ties
I've had the answer all along.

Georgina Emery (15)

In Memory Of Darren
28.12.1968 - 21.12.2005

A long hard battle you did fight
And my, you fought so well
But sadly one day, you grew so weak
And your heartbeat, it suddenly fell.
You may have lost your battle
But we are proud you fought so well.

Up there with the angels
What a wonderful place to be,
You know we all still miss you
And if only you could see,
Just how much life has changed here
For all the family and me.

Sometimes I still hear your voice
And wonder why God took you?
He gave you cancer and made you weak,
Why He did this? Not a clue.
But you'll always be remembered
For being so strong and brave too.

Up there with the angels
What a wonderful place to be,
You know we all still miss you
And if only you could see,
Just how much life has changed here
For all the family and me.

So this marks my final goodbye
And your poem, your memories, I'll keep forever . . .

Kerry Anne Wells (16)

The Pilot Of The Bleakest Sky

Waste away the endless days
On the doorstep in your home town
In the summertime
Oh it's not a pretty place to be
And all the things that you have done
You tell them to the midday sun
They drift away, ships passing in the night
The good days come to those
Who had the strength to shine on through the bad
And in the end when death is near
We'll be grateful that we persevered through the days
We lived, we laughed, we learned of the fading futures
That we yearned, it seemed so easy in our youth
Could it be further from the truth?
And truth be told, they told some lies
They left it clear within their eyes
Told tales of the things they'd seen
In places that they'd never been
The good days never came to those
The moral of the story shows
You prosper living by the rules
Give ignorance to all the fools
Waste away the endless days on a doorstep
In your hometown in the summertime
Oh it's not a pretty place to be
And all the things that you said
They formed a whirlwind in my head
Upon my mind they left a stain
The bullet took it from my brain
He rests there with the photographs
Inscribed there with the epitaphs
Which read: 'For all he could not take
They found his body in the lake
And tooth for tooth and eye for eye
The pilot of the bleakest sky
Fought solemn, bravely to the end
A cover-up, the world pretends

Disgraceful to his memory
Unjust to his humility
Gift them the sight and with their eyes
His ghost resides: in bleakest skies.

Isaac Lister (14)

War Of The World

There are times I find it hard to stop at night
We are living through such troubled times
And every child that reaches out for someone to hold
For one moment then becomes my own.
It's the war of the worlds
Every man, woman and child get ready
To fight for what you love.
It is time to be prepared, to have faith, to have love.

Chorus
I'm inspired and hopeful each and every day
That's how I know that things are gonna change.

How can I pretend that I don't know what's going on
When every second, with every minute another soul is gone.
It's the war of the worlds
Every man, woman and child get ready
To fight for what you love,
It is time to be prepared, to have faith, to have love.

Chorus
I'm inspired and hopeful each and every day
That's how I know that things are gonna change.

And it all starts right here and it starts right now.
A person stands up and the rest will follow
For all the forgotten, for all the unloved.

Chorus
I'm inspired and hopeful each and every day
That's how I know that things are gonna change.

War of the world.

Dannielle Pearce (14)

A Heart Of Black

Why do I feel this way?
So hurt, confused and lost
Because of the way you treated me
And you didn't think about the cost
A heart of black defines me
The love you took away is killing me
Why did we even start?
Why did I ever let it get that far?
Well, don't think to soothe me with nice words
Because I know who you really are
And I won't let you draw me in again
But why do I feel so empty without you
Even though I hate you?
It's not fair, why does it have to be like this?
You get away with hurting me and it hurts to see you go
A heart of black defines me and darkness is what I sink in to
Do you see what you have done to me?
Can you hear my screams?
I want you back!
Even though you may hurt me, I want you back!
I want to love you
I want you to love me
And it hurts that I can't
I see you with her
I see her with you
I see your happiness
I see what we never had
A heart of black resides in your chest
And that heart is what I want
But I can't
Because it hurts too much
I love you
But it hurts too much to love you
A heart of black surrounds me
And it is what I've become

And I can see you soaring high above me
With her
I just hope she shatters your heart
Like you did to me.

Tessa Mann (15)

Bad Day

No other things could be so worse,
Being with you would be the first.
Never been in much a mess
With you means I get much less.
Never changed my lasting frown,
Cos all the time I am so down.
(Bridge)
because of you, I cannot go the places I want to.
I cannot see the faces I want to
Let me free because . . .

(Chorus)
I'm having a bad day,
Worse than you would think.
I'm having a bad day,
Worse than words could link.

I wanna disappear into your mind,
So I can interfere, make it kind.
You never really see the sense
Watching you is sometimes tense
(Bridge)
Because of you, I cannot go the places I want to
I cannot see the faces I want to
Let me be free because . . .

(Chorus)
I'm having a bad day,
Worse than you would think.
I'm having a bad day,
Worse than words could link, yeah OK!

Lucy House (17)

Remember Me

Remember me and all we used to be
Hear this silently screaming, aching pain,
See the sadness in my eyes
All that I was or could have been
For all that you couldn't see
Close your eyes now and feel my heart break
It's not you that I don't love
It's the growing pain I cannot take.
When you feel lost, like the world is against you
Look above, there I'll be shining down
Guiding everything that you do
I don't feel this pain anymore
Life is no longer a wretched chore
I am free, I am light
I'll be your strength when you can't fight
I'll be your hope when you are low,
I'm by your side
I'll never leave
Just promise me you won't let go
Don't give them satisfaction
Show the world your love
Spread your wings and let your heart shine
Show the world your beauty, so precious, so divine
I believe in you and all that you are
My world is closer than you think
Always near, never far,
My life goes on in people like you, the people that I loved and knew. I'm not scared nor alone anymore
I'm all that you are
I'm courageous, strong and brave
I'm loved and I'm treasured
Love so golden, it can't be measured
I could have been your night and day
I would have walked beside you in your darkest hour
I have held your hand and given you my all
I'd have caught you if you fell
But my mistakes outweighed your love
I couldn't learn fast enough
Love felt too cruel life became too tough

I'm sorry that I hurt you with deepest regret and sorrow
Don't forget me, please, remember me tomorrow
Like the beginning was only yesterday
Look back and smile if only for a while.

Hetti Sansom (19)

Eclipse

Let me walk away
Run away
I want to jump
And see my star
In this lonely universe
If only Mr Moon
Could find a friend
He might shine brighter
Than the sun
Those jealous rays
Don't meet the eye
Because he's still so   unforgiving
                                    inhospitable
                                    utterly belligerent.

Open up those little eyes
There's a whole new world out there
Baby, you'll never know if you don't try
Catch a star and hitch a ride
It's not so scary when you're oh so far away . . .

Back on Earth, word is on the streets
That you've placed a bet with recklessness
Go paint the universe red
For one night only, breaking down the walls
We'll share our skies with you
Our lives with you
Everybody loves a spectacle.

Kodak's at the ready
Baby it's your spotlight.

Shona Jackson (15)

Petal

Won't you whisper to me Petal, won't you whisper?
Won't you tell me all the troubles you have seen?
Won't you tell me Lily, Lily, won't you tell me?
Won't you tell me all the places you have been?
You have seen some sights my Petal, you have seen things
Things that you are far too pretty to have seen
But you can whisper to me Petal, you can whisper
You can whisper all the places you have been.

You cry and find it frightening
When the wind has blown and blown
But when the sun is shining
How you've blossomed and you've grown
And your white petals have turned brown
The wind blows you, my dear flower
But the soil will root you down
My Lily, you're too pretty
To see the things that you have seen
But you can whisper to me Petal
All the places you have been

When the sun comes out
Reach for it
And grow as tall as you can
So when darkness falls
You'll be twice as tall
And will not need the sun

Won't you whisper to me Petal, won't you whisper?
Won't you tell me all the troubles you have seen?
Won't you tell me Lily, Lily, won't you tell me?
Won't you tell me all the places you have been?
You have seen some sights my Petal, you have seen things
Things that you are far too pretty to have seen
But you can whisper to me Petal, you can whisper
You can whisper all the places you have been.

If you whisper to me Petal, if you whisper
If you whisper al the things you wish to share
I shall listen, my dear Lily, I shall listen
I shall listen to you Petal
Cos I care.

Helen Monks (16)

Daydreaming

I sat alone in an empty room, I don't know what to do
Cos you are all I think about

I wrote a song, it's a song for you, 'bout what I should do
Cos you are all I think about

I saw your face floating in the clouds and I forget the crowds
Cos you are all I think about

I walked away from possibilities. It brings me to my knees
That you are all I think about

I'm still alone in an empty room. I know what I should do
Cos you are all I think about

My dress is on, my clothes are all brand new, so I can show to you
That you are all I think about

My tears won't show, I promise you I'll be as strong as I can be
Though you are all I think about

You're in my head, but never here with me. I know we cannot be
But you are all I think about

I'd wait a year, wait a lifetime for you (and someone else, it's true)
But you are all I think about

I'm moving on, I'm moving on from you and I'm with someone new
But you are all I think about

I won't forget how you would smile at me. That made me so happy
Cos you are all I think about

It's the last verse, it's the last line for you. I'll always think of you
Cos you are all I think about.

Jess Rushworth (15)

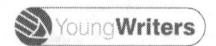

Our Forgotten Words

I always loved you with all my heart, but you didn't
I always answered your calls, but you didn't
I was always there for you, I thought you'd be there too
But you weren't, you left me alone in the cold

Why did I trust you?
Why did I care?
Was it your talent or the friendship we shared?
I miss those words you once said to me
But now those words are gone and my heart with them
I don't even remember those words.

Did you forget all the promises you gave me?
I won't ever hurt you, well I won't say that
Because my heart is broken
And every bit is with you
People have come and tried to fix me
But just when they think they've got me all patched up
They say those words we once shared
And I fall to pieces in their grip and fall back down again.

Why did I trust you?
Why did I care?
Was it your talent or the friendship we shared?
I miss those words you once said to me
But now those words are gone and my heart with them
I don't even remember those words.

I have been in the dark for so long
But now I have realised that you're not coming
And I'm following the light of my friends
They helped me through and I eventually found my way home.

I shouldn't have trusted you
I shouldn't have cared
It wasn't your talent or the friendship we shared

I remember those words you once said to me
And I have let my heart love again
But I will always love you no matter what
I'll be in the background when you need help
Just please don't forget our words . . .
I love you.

Sophie Curran (14)

Untitled?

Was my face not pretty enough?
Was my heart too broken?
Did I bore you dear?
Or was I too outspoken?

Maybe you preferred someone else
Put me on the shelf
I'll gather dust
As you live the life that I was after
My beautiful disaster

Was it something I did?
Or did you just move on?
Will I ever know what it was,
That I could do so wrong?

Maybe you preferred someone else
Put me on the shelf
I'll gather dust
As you live the life that I was after
My beautiful disaster

I don't hate you dear
(My beautiful disaster)
Cause I don't have you dear
(My beautiful disaster)
But I can't love you dear
(My beautiful disaster)
Happily ever after
My beautiful disaster.

Sophie Kelly (15)

Why?

I'm sitting on the corner of the road, all alone
Though I was alone before I heard footsteps
Hand comes down on my shoulder
Warm and friendly like
Turned around to see him staring at me

Why, oh why
Why did it have to be me?
Why, oh why?
Tell me why
Give me a reason
I need something to grasp
To hold on to.

I knew it was too good to be true
But I could not tear my eyes away
His hair so black
Eyes so brown
It was my dream come true.

Why, oh why
Why did it have to be me?
Why, oh why?
Tell me why
Give me a reason
I need something to grasp
To hold on to.

I never thought it would happen
I've never believed in fate
So I did the worst I could have done
I stood up and walked away.

Why, oh why
Why did it have to be me?
Why, oh why?

Tell me why
Give me a reason
I need something to grasp
To hold on to.

I will never forget him
Never.

Robyn-Marie Kenyon (13)

It's Not Me, It's You

You looked at me through solid brown eyes,
You said forever, it was all lies,
Then you thought whatever,
So what if she cries?
So what if she breaks down?
So what if she dies?

Your promises are broken,
Your thoughts were corrupt,
You left me heartbroken,
And if that wasn't enough . . .
You hit me, hurt me,
Trod me to the ground,
Used me, abused me,
And now I've finally found that out.

Cos our first kiss finally happened,
Then it was our last,
You gave me everything I wanted, then you took it back,
The way you held me,
I knew for a fact,
That it would last forever,
But they forgot to mention,
That facts lie.

And the sky has to cry just to fill up the river
And the sky has to cry for the sea,
And of course I would cry for my one true love,
When my one true love's not with me, not with me.

Shilpa Sisodia (15)

Jealousy

I knew you despised me all along
You brought me down, you did me wrong
And I was always good to you
I was the best and it was true.

For all the good things that I had
There was venom in your heart
You saw the potential I had
And tried to tear me apart.

Jealousy, jealousy
Why are you so jealous of me?
Jealousy, jealousy
Why are you so jealous of me?

You were a leach upon my skin
Drawing blood out, to put failure in
Kicking, scratching, fighting me
Hindering what I was meant to be.

For all the good things that I had
There was venom in your heart
You saw the potential I had
And tried to tear me apart.

Jealousy, jealousy
Why are you so jealous of me?
Jealousy, jealousy
Why are you so jealous of me?

Your words, they have made me strong
Pulling me down has helped me along
Like a phoenix back from the black ashes
I've risen without any backlashes.

For all the good things that I had
There was venom in your heart
You saw the potential I had
And tried to tear me apart.

Jealousy, jealousy
Why are you so jealous of me?
Jealousy, jealousy
Why are you so jealous of me?

Jordaine Henningham (15)

Star-Crossed Lovers

Intro (just talking)
If I could just be with you
I'd cling onto you all my life
Being with you makes me so content
My body can flee from the strife.

Verse 1
Yes, our parents disagree, they fight
But that doesn't make me love you less
Let's not let them destroy what we have
They'll just make our lives a mess.

Bridge
Come on we've got to stay together
If someone's got a problem they have to live with it - forever.

Chorus
We just can't run away and hide from this
We were made as a match
Meant to be pieced together by fate
They've gotta believe us
Star-crossed lovers
Star-crossed lovers.

Verse 2
The ancient grudge must fly on by
And never to be lifted again
Buried beneath the earth it should lie
So for us Romeo there's no pain.

Bridge
Chorus.

Vicki Good (14)

River Of Broken Hearts

The time has come to evaluate
My heart is already broken and it's way too late
I find it hard even just to smile
Because moving on was never my style
I'm gonna have to face it, that there is no more us
But my heart just cannot take it, the reason is because

I lost the one thing, the someone that I needed
I lost the only thing in which I had succeeded

I'm drifting down the river of broken hearts
I'm still hurting about what tore us apart
Although I know for sure, what we had was strong before
But my heart wants to move on, a feeling I can't ignore.

Although you left some time ago
I still feel your presence, perhaps that may still show
And when I see you, memories flood my thoughts
Most will remain good, despite that some will not.

I don't want to open my heart, to let it break again
But when you love someone,
It's a feeling you must not defend.

I'm drifting down the river of broken hearts
I'm still hurting about what tore us apart
Although I know for sure, what we had was strong before
But my heart wants to move on, a feeling I can't ignore.

When I do find someone who's gonna love me right
My heart can stop yearning, perhaps I'll now sleep at night?

I'm drifting down the river of broken hearts
I'm still hurting about what tore us apart
Although I know for sure, what we had was strong before
But my heart wants to move on, a feeling I can't ignore.

I'm drifting down the river of broken hearts
I'm still hurting about what tore us apart
Although I know for sure, what we had was strong before
But my heart wants to move on, a feeling I can't ignore.

Although I can still taste your kiss
This heartache is what I will not miss.

Scott McCutcheon (16)

No More Hating

They got me on my knees
Saying, 'Oh God.'
I know I keep it goin'
But these times are so hard
It's moments like this
That you're a little scarred

Life's gettin' harder and harder
But I gotta keep it real
Not gettin' down on my knees
No, I'm not gonna conceal
No, I'm not runnin' away
Not gonna hide how I feel

No way, I ain't takin' no more
I'm with the girl I adore
But you still hatin' on me
Yo man, you're startin' to bore
The living life outta me
This trash you gotta ignore

I'm making a stand
I'm breaking free
Not gonna be pushed around
Nope, I'm being the new me
It's time to stand up
And show you all who I really am
So bye-bye, I'll see you later
I ain't gonna take another hater.

Dale Manning (16)

The City Light Dancers

Stare into the depths and wonder
Turn slowly, don't let anyone steal your thunder
Step away from the railings
And do not admit to your failings
One hand on the cold steel
One hand making sure this is real
Tell yourself what they told you before
And cover up what lies at your core

Look out over the river
And find all your answers
As the wind bites, you shiver
Surrounded by all the city light dancers

You've been stopped many times in the past
Try so hard but nothing seems to last
Now you feel so exhausted and want to rest
Back in your prime you slogged it out with the best
The murky water starts to call you
And you have to do what you have to do
Glance over the railings and make up your mind
It's not too hard when you know what you'll find

Look out over the river
And find all your answers
As the wind bites, you shiver
Surrounded by all the city light dancers

Lean back and look up into the sky
And wish and hope you will fly that high
Push yourself and know that you can't look back
The struggle's ending now but still you can't be slack
Your body sullenly defies your brain
All you want to do is to end the pain
Surrounded by dancers on your last day
Nobody sees you slowly slip away.

Look out over the river
And find all your answers
As the wind bites, you shiver
Surrounded by all the city light dancers

Tom Nixon (15)

Who You Are (Beat Of Your Heart)

Listen to the beat of the drums
Listen to the strumming of guitars
It doesn't matter what we want
As long as you understand
Listen to the beat of your heart
You can't lose it
The beat of your heart
You can use it
No matter how wide or far
Listen to the beat of your heart
It doesn't matter if you're on a star
You can use it
It will show you who you are
Even if you fly away
It will be there
As high as the sky
It's who you are
You can't lose it
Cos it's there for you
When you need it
The beat of your heart
Just listen to the beat of your heart
As long as you use it
You can't lose it
It's who you are
Listen to the bet of the drums
Listen to the strumming of guitars
As long as you've got what you need
You will know who you are!

Eleanor Gregory (13)

Untitled

When I was at the end of ten
I thought my life was hard enough
Doing homework again and again
Is *hardly* fun stuff

Going to school six hours a day
Aching butt and a half-asleep attitude
No one cares about the other essay
And no one gives a sign of gratitude.

I wish every day could be my day
Have everything my way
Do whatever I want
When I want
Freedom blows through the air
Anything happens without a care
That's the way I like it.

Oh yeah

I wish every day could be my day
Have everything my way
Do whatever I want
When I want
Freedom blows through the air
Anything happens without a care
That's the way I like it.

Oh, oh, oh, yeah

Guitar solo

I was every day was a fun day
Playing football on a runway
Doing what I want
When I want
Freedom flies my way.

Doing what I want when I want
Doing what I want when I want
Doing what I want when I want
Oh yeah
That's what I call living.

Jack Fenton (15)

Butterfly

Well the world goes by
So slowly
Like a butterfly
I'm lonely
Now please tell me why
I bother
Like a butterfly
You hover
With myself and I
I wander
Like a butterfly
I ponder
On the ways of life
It flutters like a butterfly.

I look into your eyes
There's no feeling
Like a butterfly
You're still healing
How do I get this right?
Without hurting
Like a butterfly
I'm still learning
I think me, oh my
What am I doing?
Like a butterfly
I need soothing
Because love is not a lie
It flutters like a butterfly.

Hazel Gambles (13)

Netball Matches

(Tune Bohemian Rhapsody)

Is this a real match? Or is this fantasy?
Come on Crohamians, we must bring victory!
Open your eyes, look up to the skies and see!
We're just the B team, give us your sympathy . . .
Because we work so hard on Wednesdays and we're giving you this display
Anywhere the ball goes doesn't really matter to us . . . we still lose

Mama, just lost a match
Croydon High just took the ball, so we couldn't shoot at all
Mama, season had just begun and now we've gone and thrown the chance away
Mama, ohhh, ohhh, ohhh
We couldn't catch the ball even though we really leapt,
We couldn't do it, we couldn't do it, we couldn't do it and now the season's over!

I see the shadow of a Croydon High girl,
Will she shoot? Is it in? Have we lost by miles?
Oh dreary me, I think we can see we've lost . . .
Blow the whistle, blow the whistle, blow the whistle umpire
Go on and blow

We're just the B team, nobody loves us (they're just the B team nobody loves them)
Spare us a match against Croydon High

And we catch and we throw but we can't shoot a goal
Oh no, they cannot get a goal (yes we can)
Oh no, they cannot get a goal (yes we can)
Mrs Hammond, Mrs Hammond please Miss, please don't make us go,
We're unprepared, we're scared and we're going to freeze
To freeze, to frreeeeeeezzzzeeeeee

So you think you can win the watch every time,
So you think you can pull Sophie's hair from behind
Oh chavs, you hurt her real bad, you're out of the match so go and get the bus home

We're not always winners but we're still a team,
We'll be strong together cos winning doesn't matter to us!

Michela Scarpa & Lauren Santana (17)

The Lonely Road

The deserted island on which I live
My heart left feeling cold
The tears are falling down my face
Unable to leave a single trace
My emotions torn and twisted
Wrote down in a book was listed.

Walking down a lonely road
With no one's hand to hold.

Our time together was a blast
But nothing seems to ever last
The beads of joy around my neck
The glint in your eye
The shine of your smile
Reflected upon mile and mile.

Walking down a lonely road
With no one's hand to hold.

The hidden truth blurred by my vision
Was where you held the final decision
This was the end, there was no future
No love in which to depend
No way forward
And no way back
My life's decision is what I lack.

Walking down a lonely road
With no one's hand to hold.

Amy Louise Jones (15)

Rain On My Head

Can you hear the sound of deep rolling thunder?
Can you only stare and wonder?
Blue raindrops keep falling down my face
Running fast as if for a race
Can you taste the bitter-sweet memories
Can you touch those crisp golden leaves?
Can you smell that sweet green grass?
But that's all, that's just the past
You're gone now, gone forever
And that's it. We'll never be together
Touch my hand, baby don't let me go
Cos I need you, I love you so
Oh I wish you didn't go away on that cold and dark October day
Knew something was wrong
Too late, you were gone
Fire rose from the burning blaze
You never woke up from that smoky haze
At night I still hear you whispering sweet words in my ear
I wake up and realise you're not near
I'm calling, shouting out your name
No answer, life's never gonna be the same
I can't go on living without you
Darling you know it's true
I can't help it; I'm still madly in love with you

Harsh winds whip around me lashing
My train of thoughts keeps on crashing
If only I could turn back time
I'd walk down that line
Take you back where you belong
You wouldn't have gone
Could have saved you from dying
Then I wouldn't be here crying
Those beautiful almond-shaped eyes
Never did look so surprised
The doctors said you wouldn't cope
But I never gave up hope

Oh this road is gonna be so long
Now that my moon has gone
Didn't realise how much you were worth
Until you left this forsaken Earth
I can hear the turning of a key
But there's no one here, just me
There's your shadow in the hall
Standing straight, standing tall
Come softly towards the mirror
Lemme see you one last time before you disappear
Deep into the bewitching night
Where stars shine for you bright
Bring me back from broken dreams
Step into the splintered sunlight.

Kirsty Johnston (19)

Look Into The Distance

Look into the distance, what can you see?
Look further than anyone has looked before
A big blue moon and a lovely sea
Lots of little fish swimming in the sea
A big brown owl sitting on that tree
And that is what I can see

Look into the distance, what can you see?
Look further than anyone has done before
Great big clouds floating in the air
Lovely brown rabbits hopping over there
Hopping away from that big brown bear
That is all I can see.

Cameron Donaghy (11) & Ashley Donaghy (13)

I Have A Song

You are the hero in my story
You are the hero everywhere
You might want to give up
You might miss home

I will walk with you
When you are all alone
With so much unknown
Along the way

I promise I'll carry you
When you need a friend
When you are weary
You know I'll be there
Because you can feel me
When I say I am there for you

I will walk with you
When you are all alone
With so much unknown
Along the way

When your heart is full of sadness and despair
I will carry you
When you need a friend
I will be there.

I will walk with you
When you are all alone
With so much unknown
Along the way

So keep going
You're nearly there
I will walk with you
When you are all alone
With so much unknown
Along the way.

Natalie Dickinson (13)

Hello There Friend

You are the source of my signature, the Source of my pain
No matter how much I hurt you, I have nothing to gain
'Cause you're wasting my time, by wasting mine
I find it hard to breathe - you're pushing down on me.

(Bridge)
You're in my shadow
You're in my mirror
You're in the reflection - on the blades and the knife
I want you to leave, yet you are my life.

(Chorus)
Hello there, 'friend' did you miss me?
When I was in my subconscious slumber
Bleeding, screaming and hurting - why?
(Because you told me to)
Is it a surprise that I hate you?
Who are you? Living my life
The life that you made me try to end with a knife
I look in the mirror - you're not worthy of my tears
I smash that mirror - it's exposed my fears
You're living my life, living my life
'Cause
(Bridge)
You're living my life . . . taking my life!
(Chorus)
Life support machine bleeps and you hear doctors speaking
Silence
You've taken my life!
Music starts again . . .
Hello there, 'friend' did you miss me?
When I was in my subconscious slumber
Bleeding, screaming and hurting - why?
(Because you told me to)
Is it a surprise . . . that I killed you?

Nicole Leigh Topham (15)

Colours Back Tonight

It gets a little lonely
When you're not around
It's like when you're not here
I can't see colour or hear sound.
All of my memories play in black and white,
I really hope to get my colours back tonight.

Chorus 1
It gets a little frightening,
A little bit exciting.
How am I gonna see
When you're standing next to me?
If all I see is black and white,
I gotta get my colours back tonight.

It gets a little scary
When you leave me on my own.
It's like a million miles from home.
All of my dreams take place in black and white,
I really want to get my colours back tonight.

Chorus 2
I get a little stronger
If I hold you a little longer.
I'm finally starting to see,
That you're almost next to me.
In this world of black and white,
I've almost got my colours back tonight.

Chorus 3
Well now you can see I'm happy.
Happy with what I see.
I see you standing next to me,
And there's no more black and white,
I finally got my colours back tonight.
Yeah, I finally got my colours back tonight.

Katy Brown (15)

I Asked You Nicely

I'm waiting here for you to call me
It's the smile upon your face that makes me smile
I'm sitting here in the rainfall
Please come down from Heaven now
I ask you please.

Why did you have to go?
I know it's a challenge for you and me
I said to take it slow
I asked you nicely.

I'm wondering why I ever thought I loved you
It's probably cos you said you'll always love me
I can't believe that I trusted you
You said we'll always be together until we die.

Why did you have to go?
I know it's a challenge for you and me
I said to take it slow
I asked you nicely.

Didn't I give you enough
I thought I gave you whatever you wanted
Baby, I don't understand
Please come and take my hand
I've always loved you
So let me say

Why did you have to go?
I know it's a challenge for you and me
I said to take it slow
I asked you nicely.

Why did you have to go?
I know it's a challenge for you and me
I said to take it slow
I asked you nicely.

Nicole Robinson (14)

Hear My Footsteps

I'll live my life while it lives me
But death follows me everywhere I go
They say I'm untouchable
But I don't know
We don't know enough about life to die
Why can't we go on until we're done
We never know when it's gonna claim us
But we all continue toward the setting sun

Chorus

When I'm gone
When I go wherever they go
You will hear my footsteps
Every time the wind blows

Can death be worse than life?
Will we ever know?
All our questions go unanswered
When people are gone where do they go?
Why do we care?
Why do we fret?
We all think about it but why?
Can't it be that what you see is what you get?

Chorus

When we get old we know what to do
We rock the house and wait for the Reaper
We don't slow down
We leave that to the timekeeper
Because what's waiting for us on the other side can wait
It ain't over till it's over
And that's called fate
Until the day we die, we hold tight to our four-leafed clover.

Chorus x 2.

Daniel Keith

Diversity

I may not be a social bunny
Or a queen bee
But I can deal with that.

I am a lone wolf with my own style
And character
So I could lead a pack.

You may mock me, tease me, provoke me,
Even maim me
And yet I'm still myself.

I'm not your typical girl.
I'm not your regular girl.
I'm not your usual girl
But I don't care what you say.

Who cares what I'm like?
Who cares what I do?
Who cares who I am?
That's diversity for you!

I guess I don't wear a plastic mask,
A fake ego
And lie about myself.

I'd rather be me than an icon
Of false fame and pride
For they have ugly minds.

You may mock me, tease me, taunt me but
Nothing will change
'Cause I love me for me!

I'm not your typical girl.
I'm not your regular girl.
I'm just an original girl
And I don't care what you say.

Emily Whittingham (15)

Have Faith

Hey, don't be upset
'Cause it's not the end
I know he hurt you
And that you took the offence
But reality is tough like a stab in the wound
Once you dealt with it you can get through.

But if you suddenly feel like wasting your dreams
'Cause you got nothing left in your heart
Then you'll for sure be living the rest of your life
In the harsh cold world of the dark
Do you really want to give up life?
Don't you want a brand new start?
Because you're never too late to do it again
You know you're tougher than you think you are
Just have faith, faith, faith
Just have faith.

Time is all it takes
A very precious thing
If you use it well
The rewards will gladly last
Happiness happens if you give it the chance
But emotions can return from the past.

You can see your life change and it won't cost a thing
'Cause it all comes from your heart
Just give it a shot by knowing what you got
And you'll be right back on your guard
But this is all up to you
You're in control of your life
Because you're never too late to start again
You know you're tougher than you think you are
Just have faith, faith, faith
Just have faith.

Tiffany Ching (15)

Woe Tea

You say that we should sort out our lives
But our problems are not solved with high-fives
Then you said that we should lie low
But you called me an idiot, so I told you to go.

We tried so much to sort out our troubles
With Haagen-Dazs and 'Bath 'n' Bubbles'
Opera music and sexy clothes
Gardening and evening shows
Nothing works out anymore
The spark is gone and that's our flaw.

But the arguments go on and on and on and on and on

Sit back, relax and drink your 'Woe Tea'
'Cause you're complaining's bothering me
Some things you say are discriminatory
When I want cider, you want your 'Woe Tea'
Want a biscuit to go with your hot beverage
'Cause our relationship needs a little leverage?
Quick everyone, we've all got to leave
For she's gone and made herself another mug of her 'Woe Tea'.

I've lost my concentration
For it's her determination
To sign my termination
Just for a celebration
Girl, you have made me stress
It is you who made this mess
Now you should really confess
I'll let these words say the rest.

Oh, it's just the way it goes, my friends tell me
Oh, it's only tea
Oh, but I say back at them
It's not the tea itself, it's what it represents.

Aaron Parr (15)

Vampire

I would love to be a vampire
Pale-skinned and fast
As much blood as I desire
My life would be a blast

Are they real or unreal?
That's for you to decide
Do what you feel
Even if it's run and hide

Are you willing
To see your family cry?
As blood's not that filling
Even once you die

To become a creature of the night
Let yourself be taken
Will you give up your life without a fight?
You will then enter the vampire's haven

Then a vampire bit me
And turned me into a vampire
I was in such misery
I now live in the vampire's empire

The vampire venom
Will then rage and surge
Through my arteries
And my nerves

So now I am a vampire
Pale-skinned and fast
As much blood as I desire
My life will be a blast

I love being a vampire
With all my vampire heart.

Kiera Whitbread

That's The Thing With Irony

She never thought they could be
She said, 'A boy like him
Could never love a girl like me
He don't even know my name
But I guess I'm the one to blame
Cos I never tried to say hello
And I know if I ask him out he would say no.'

You see that's the thing with irony
Cos that boy loved her secretly
He watched her each day
On the way to school
On the bus, on the train.

He never thought they could be
He said, 'A girl that pretty
Could never fall for a waster like me
She don't even know my name
She could never feel the same
Cos I never tried to say hello
And if I asked for her number she would say no.'

You see that's the thing with irony
Cos that boy loved her secretly
He watched her each day
On the way to school
On the bus, on the train.

They never got together
Even though they had feelings
That could have lasted forever
You see that's the thing with irony
They both loved each other secretly
Secretly
Secretly.

Bethany Foley (17)

Opposites Attract

Do you really think we'd be a pair?
Mud on your clothes,
Hay in your hair.

Do you think that marriage is for us?
Me in my limo,
You on the bus.

You're just a farm boy,
And I'm a model Gucci girl,
A new pair of shoes has my head in a whirl.
We'll never be. Oh so sorry

Then I saw you again one day,
Without the Gucci glasses,
Followed by the paparazzi
Blinded by camera flashes.
And you said:

'I'm not just a farm lad,
I've tried to say before,
Now I'll be your A-list boy,
You'll want me even more.
I love you, oh, not sorry.
I'll take you to dinner,
At your favourite place,
And I'll even pay the prices
Of a dress at Versace.'

I was so wrong at the start,
And now you, boy, have my heart,
Oh my darling farmer boy.

And from now on I'll make it a fact,
The truth in romance
is that opposites attract.

Jessica Frost (14)

Just Smile!

Smile when you're happy
Smile when you're glad
Smile when you laugh
Smile even if you're sad.

Just smile, just smile
So the world can see you smile
Just smile, just smile
So everybody can join in and smile!

Smile when the sunshine is out
Smile if you are feeling down
Smile when everyone's about
Smile when you're in town.

Just smile, just smile
So the world can see you smile
Just smile, just smile
So everybody can join in and smile!

Smile when your friends are upset
Smile at the people you meet
Smile at the people you've met
Smile when somebody tickles your feet.

Just smile, just smile
So the world can see you smile
Just smile, just smile
So everybody can join in and smile!

Just smile, just smile
So the world can see you smile
Just smile, just smile
So everybody can join in and smile
So everybody can join in and smile
Just smile.

Hannah Mereweather (13)

Super Race!

Peace, love whatever man,
We're not all hippy dippy,
We just want a better life,
Without fighting, without war!

Just give up your weapons, you know you can.
War is not good, it's not cool,
If we help each other peace will rule,
Just picture the faces of the free,
Work with me and you will see.

We don't want no fuss,
But yeah, we want peace,
No death, no tears,
No hurting inside,
The world so far is not enough.

War is not good, it's not cool,
If we help each other peace will rule,
Just picture the faces of the free,
Walk with me and you will see.

They say we're crazy,
That we don't see,
A world without war
Would be better for all.

War is not good, it's not cool,
If we help each other peace will rule,
Just picture the faces of the free,
Walk with me and you will see.

A world without war
A super race
Peace will reign
For evermore.

Jennifer Downing (13)

Why?

Why does life keep coming back
And hitting me in the face?
It's getting me crazy

Got to get up today
Forget what people say
It doesn't matter
But I can't keep that in my head
They make me fall
It makes me hurt

How come it's always me?
Am I the only one
They have their eye on?
Their words are hurting me bad

Got to get up today
Forget what people say
It doesn't matter
But I can't keep that in my head
They make me fall
It makes me hurt

Not a supernatural thing
And I've got to get this thing off
And stab it in the back

Got to get up today
Forget what people say
It doesn't matter
But I can't keep that in my head
They make me fall
It makes me hurt
I just need it to
Stop!

Lauren Hay (14)

The End?

Did it have to end like this?
It only started yesterday!
Was that the final kiss?
And then you went away!

What was wrong with me?
What was wrong with us?
Did you really have to go?
Was it not enough
That you had my love?
How could you ever be so low?

Now alone what shall I do?
Guess my love for you still strong!
Should I just move on
Or should I stick with you?

What was wrong with me?
What was wrong with us?
Did you really have to go?
Was it not enough
That you had my love?
How could you ever be so low?

I suppose this is the end
My future's looking down!
No hope for me at all!
And my heart is broken now!

I know what was wrong with me
And what was wrong with us
And it was best for us to part
You always had my love
But it proved not enough
You hurt me from the start.

Katiey Alice Vine (14)

Locked Hearts

Touching your hand back then, that's when I knew
That forgetting you would be so hard
Why did you have to go make that mistake?
Causing me horror that's . . .
Breaking me apart.

Whenever I see your face
I wish our love was an embrace
Always shining and shining
Like an everlasting star
But I know you'll be my dark, locked heart.

Living a depressing, boring life
You being with me, brings it alive
Why do you now reach out for my hand?
Giving me hopes that . . .
Maybe, we could try again.

Whenever I see your face
I wish our love was an embrace
Always shining and shining
Like an everlasting star
But I know you'll be my dark, locked heart.

As our bodies are moving closer now
We see each other's flames arise
Feeling the passion, we know something's true
Freeing the fire, we . . .
Share our first kiss.

Whenever I see your face
I wish our love was an embrace
Always shining and shining
Like an everlasting star
But I know you'll be my dark, locked heart.

Michelle Neal (16)

She Was Perfect

Back in the old school
There was only one love for me
You will never guess who it would be
She was a beautiful girl
Smart as can be
It's not just her looks it's her personality.

She was perfect, face reality
She's gone now, she's moved on, she's married to he
He was my best friend
As jealousy takes over me

From time to time I thought she loved me
But I just knew it was never to be
I kept on trying but then I gave in
Because then I knew I was never gonna win
My best friend came and told me he loved her
I don't know what he sees in her
Because she's a total player

She was perfect, face reality
She's gone now, she's moved on, she's married to he
He was my best friend
As jealousy takes over me

I said all that now but I don't mean it
I have been a total idiot
I have been fooled now my best friend has taken her
Jealousy is here I have to get rid of it
It's been so long now, I loved her more
Because she was the girl I really adored

She was perfect, face reality
She's gone now, she's moved on, she's married
Oh she was perfect.

Matthew Davenport & Robert Bond (12)

Paper Toys

I spent my day making paper snowflakes
Then I watched as they flew up and away
Now I'm wondering where my old dreams went
And if it was you that led them astray

But it's easy for me
To just blame it all on you
And it's easy for you
To just blame it all on me
But it's hard for us
To just say what we mean

Cos I just want to feel your hand in mine
Feel your heartbeat and listen to you feel mine
Watch your eyes close as you fall asleep
And as I imagine you lying there, I weep

I made some paper dolls that looked like us
Revenge is sweet so I tore your head right off
But guilt came knocking at my door again
Here's your funeral, then I'll write you off

But it's easy for me
To just blame it all on you
And it's easy for you
To just blame it all on me
But it's hard for us
To just say what we mean

Cos I just want to feel your hand in mind
Feel your heartbeat and listen to you feel mine
Watch your eyes close as you fall asleep
And as I imagine you lying there, I weep
I watch your eyes close as you fall asleep
And as I imagine you lying there, I weep.

Helena Clough (15)

Getting Over You

To wake up and know one day you are gone
And to feel everything is wrong,
I've never felt so lost and afraid
And wonder some days what went wrong?
The day you told me we were through
My heart broke in two
As if you know how I feel,
I sometimes wonder if my heart will ever heal,
Some days are good, some days are bad
But when it's raining I am sad.
I look at you and see you're fine,
What happened during our time?
My friends told me he was wrong
But I thought you were the one.
You made me feel like I belonged,
When you held me I felt safe,
Like nothing in this world
Could separate us.
When you kissed me I wasn't afraid anymore,
But now you're gone
I don't know what is real and what's a dream.
I was so happy when we were together
It's hard to forget you,
But I'm gonna try to move on with my life
I will eventually get better once you're out of my life,
Though it will feel weird, I guess we need to try
To move on for the best,
Getting over you is hard to do
But with a little time the pain will go
And I will show it some day
And you will think back and wonder
What an idiot you were to let me go.

Jennifer Glover (15)

Let's Rock

I sing this song all day long
Rockin' and rollin' just poppin' along
Come on baby just sing along
Up in my tree house playing along

Chorus
Let's rock
Come on baby please just rock along

Every girl that passes me
Baby I don't care you gotta see
Baby you gotta believe in me
That you're the only one for me

Chorus
Let's rock
Come on baby please just rock along

Come on baby please just rock along
I know you don't believe in me
Come on baby then you will see
Yh, yh baby just you and me

Chorus
Let's rock
Come on baby please just rock along

You are a pretty young thing
You gotta see
When you moved next door to me
I did not know what to say
Come on baby come to play

Chorus
Let's rock
Come on baby please just rock along

Simon Ball (14)

The Angels Cried

I remember when I first saw you
I thought my soul would rip in two
Your beauty cut me like a knife
I knew from then you'd save my life
But then you went and broke my heart
With innocent lover's killing art
The moon was shattered, the stars died
And up in Heaven, the angels cried.

I know I've got myself to blame
I was a ghost before you came
Forgive me for my selfish sin
Come back to me, we can live again
I've never been in love before
Don't say that you don't feel this sure
There's nothing else that's worth this pain
I know I'll never love again.

The truth I see shine in your eyes
Pure enough to make angels cry
Never change the angel that you are
Being with you felt like kissing stars
When poets grieve and children fear
No celestial being sheds a tear
But when you left me here to die
I swear to God, the angels cried.

Standing outside the old hotel
The rain is freezing, I can't tell

If love's a trap, I don't want freeing
If love's a curse, then let it be
If love's a song, then I'll keep singing
And let the angels cry for me.

Holly Thwaites-Bee (16)

My Very First

Every time it feels like I'm under pressure
You're saying you love me but I know that ain't true
If it really was then why is she with you?
You text me all night saying don't give up on us
Damn you, you don't really care, there is no trust
So let me say one thing
I love you more than she ever could and you know that.

There's no trust, there is nothing anymore
You picked her over us, there ain't nothing anymore
You gave up a long time ago
And you put on a stupid face for show
But you were my very first teenage crush,

You'll never know how much I cared
You thought I would forget you
And you were wishing you would forget me too
Certain things about me you hated
So it was me that you traded
Blonde hair, blue eyes
I've never seen someone look so familiar

There's no trust, there is nothing anymore
You picked her over us, there ain't nothing anymore
You gave up a long time ago
And you put on a stupid face for show
But you were my very first teenage crush,

One day I had it all
The next it was all yours
So what does that leave me with?
My very first teenage heartbreak?
But I guess it's because you're my
Very first teenage crush.

Joanna Henshall (14)

Missing Piece

The sun shines all for you
Guiding you through darkness
The flowing river reflects
Our love in the moonlit night
I dream of you all day through
With you by my side
A love you cannot hide

I'm sick of waiting for that day
The day when I look into your eyes
And get that feeling
You're the missing piece
The missing piece
The missing piece
The missing piece to my heart

It's lonely here without you
Sitting in this small room
All there is is the memories you left behind
The phone lays beside me
Waiting for you to call me
So that I hear you voice once more
All I know is that I love you, that's for sure.

I'm sick of waiting for that day
The day when I look into your eyes
And get that feeling
You're the missing piece
The missing piece
The missing piece
The missing piece to my heart

I'm sick of waiting for that day
You're the missing piece.

Sarah Hughes (16)

I'll Prove You Wrong

Sometimes I feel like the whole world hates me
And sometimes I try to forget who I wanna be
But deep down I know
That even though they don't think so
I'm gonna make it

Doubt and failure are the two things I dread
When I lie here alone, trying to think in my head
For you see there is no place I'd rather be
Than on the big screen or the home TV

Well this is my dream
This is who I wanna be
And if you don't think I can make it
I'll just prove you wrong
And this is my style
To be famous for at least a while
And if you don't think I can make it
I'll just prove you wrong

At school they all laugh
And say I'll never be like that
I'll never be the girl
That is known by the world
And I try to block out
Their criticisms and doubt
And hold in the urge to stand up and shout

Well this is my dream
This is who I wanna be
And if you don't think I can make it
I'll just prove you wrong
I'll just prove you wrong
'Cause I am strong.

Amy Cooper (13)

That Secret Boy

Your eyes, they sparkle
You see the real me
How am I supposed to leave
When it's you I love so deep?
I see you, the butterflies they jump
There you are, I feel drunk
I can't remember a thing
Then I see you look up
A frenzy of feelings begin.

You look at me, but do you see
Who I am, the inner me?
Walking towards me, my heart just beats
You're getting closer, I feel sick
You're just running through my mind
I just want you to be mine.

I want to tell you how I feel
But I don't want to get hurt again
How can I tell you I love you so
When you're practically my boy best friend?
How can you not see you belong with me?

Do you know you're breaking my heart
I'm wearing right there on my sleeve?
You might as well just go and stab it
It would hurt a lot less than these feelings.

You look at me, but do you see
Who I am, the inner me?
Walking towards me, my heart just beats
You're getting closer, I feel sick
You're just running through my mind
I just want you to be mine.

Demi Peters (15)

Wait

Sometimes at night I stay awake
To see if you will call
But now for weeks, I haven't slept
No word from you at all
I pass the place where we first met
You still don't have a clue
Even though there is no word
I live and breathe for you.

Though the silence haunts me
I will wait and see
If in fact you truly love her
Or if you'll fall for me
We'll wait for days to see
If this could be our fate
But I guess I'll have to wait.

There can be times when I am mad
With your naivety
You sit and think of you and her
And I of you and me
But through our laughs and crazy jokes
Along with all we do
It's incredible you can't see
I really do love you.

Though the silence haunts me
I will wait and see
If in fact you truly love her
Or if you'll fall for me
We'll wait for days to see
If this could be our fate
But I guess I'll have to wait.

Katie Burton (13)

MySpace Is Dying

What will I do without you?
Because you're dying
I am trying
But everyone else is switching
They are leaving you
I don't know what to do.

Because MySpace
Is my place
But Facebook and Twitter
They're making you look bitter

I want to stay
But I'm afraid one day
I'll be the only one
And MySpace will be done.

Because MySpace
Is my place
But Facebook and Twitter
They're making you look bitter

MySpace is prettier
But everyone prefers Facebook and Twitter
But you will always be the one for me
MySpace show them what you can be
Because MySpace
Is my place
But Facebook and Twitter
They're making you look bitter

What will I do without you?
Because everyone has gone
And I'm afraid MySpace is done!

Hayley Wragg (16)

It's Time To Be You

Sometimes you feel like you're all alone
Like nobody understands you
Stay up in your room all day
Nothing to do and nowhere to go.

Well, come out of that shell and jump around
Let loose and turn the music up real loud
Rock out and grab that microphone
Speak out and play your favourite tune
It's time to be you.

Keep your headphones on all day
Block out whatever they have to say
Be one with yourself
Don't let anybody tell you that that's wrong

Well, come out of that shell and jump around
Let loose and turn the music up real loud
Rock out and grab that microphone
Speak out and play your favourite tune
It's time to be you.

It's time to be you
People talk and friends in fights
You try to avoid all your frights
But maybe it's time to just be yourself

Well, come out of that shell and jump around
Let loose and turn the music up real loud
Rock out and grab that microphone
Speak out and play your favourite tune
It's time to be you
It's time to be you
So just break out.

Anfernee Duncombe (13)

Bewildered Adolescent

I want to be alone so come and sit with me,
We'll talk about the good times beneath the apple tree.
There are things you don't know, but then neither do I,
So let's just sit and think about them, below the deep blue sky.

Oh why are there always questions - never answers?
Why is life so confusing - my mind just wonders?
How am I supposed to breathe, when you're my oxygen?
My only ray of sun
You were the only one
And now that you have gone . . .

I try to think about, how the world could be
If people lived together, in perfect harmony
This world will never change, I guess it's just a fact
That below the shiny surface is a prison still in-tact

Oh why are there always questions - never answers?
Why is life so confusing - my mind just wonders?
How am I supposed to breathe, when you're my oxygen?
My only ray of sun
You were the only one
And now that you have gone . . .

Some people never search, further than their minds,
To find out if their heart agrees with the rest of Earth's mankind.
They just keep living on - smiling cheek to cheek,
Whilst within they are just begging, their destinys to seek.

Oh now, I realise that life is not a game, and I,
Do not want to wander, beyond my deep green bed,
Which lies beneath the tree,
With you right next to me, I may begin to see
I'm who I want to be.

Amy Wootton

I'll Be Rockin'!

I'll be rockin'
Don't move your lips, lips
Shake your hips, hips
Take your time, time
And you can shine, shine
I'm in the room while you're looking
I can see it now come booking
I don't waste time so bust this life
So go, go and see me . . .
Bust it, break it, feel it, move it
If that is the way that the beats will play
Just say, I will be doin' it my way
The beats are pumping
The crowd is jumping
Feel the noise
And you can hear my voice
Let's do it like there's no tomorrow
Sing it, play it, without no sorrow
Bust it, break it, feel it, move it
If that's the way the beats will play
Just say
I'm doing it my way
If only we can see
This track was made for you and me
Just unlock it with your key and . . .
Bust it, break it, feel it, move it
If that's the way the beat will play . . .
Just say . . .
Just say
I'll be doin' it my way . . .
And feel it!

India Collen (13)

Bursting Bubbles

I was walking along the street

Bursting bubbles with the people I meet
Walking in the city everywhere
Because that is what I do!

I'm bursting bubbles everywhere I walk (I walk)
Like the dreams in my heart (happy dreams)
I'm bursting bubbles like you've never seen before (before)
Bursting bubbles, the law can't stop me
It's a free country, the law can't stop me.

I was skipping in the village
Bursting bubbles every time I touch the road
Skipping around the block
Because that it what I do!

I'm bursting bubbles everywhere I walk (I walk)
Like the dreams in my heart (happy dreams)
I'm bursting bubbles like you've never seen before (before)
Bursting bubbles, the law can't stop me
It's a free country, the law can't stop me.

I was jogging in the town
Bursting bubbles every time I smiled
Jogging round the shops
Because that is what I do!

I'm bursting bubbles everywhere I walk (I walk)
Like the dreams in my heart (happy dreams)
I'm bursting bubbles like you've never seen before (before)
Bursting bubbles, the law can't stop me
It's a free country, the law can't stop me.

Bursting bubbles!

Amie Shave (11)

A Better Person - Dream, Believe, Achieve

Aimee has a baby;
Who she has to care for daily,
But her letterbox is filling up with bills.
She's never had a family,
And her baby has no daddy,
But she's got to face her problems and be real.
She waits around a corner;
For a passing car to call her,
And she makes a little money for her rent.
Even though she's suicidal;
She still really loves her child,
So she's praying hard to God to give her help.

She said, 'Lord I wanna change my life
I wanna be a better person.
Don't leave me standing in the rain
Please let me be a better person.
I know I've done a lot of wrong
I know I've failed you in the past,
But Lord I'm gonna change my life;
I'm gonna be a better person.'

Now Aimee is successful;
She says God has been so faithful,
And she has her own beauty hair salon.
Her baby's gotten older;
And is now a playful toddler
He is glad to never have to be alone.
The moral of this story;
Is that you should never worry,
Because God will always be right by your side.
Yes God will always be right by your side.

Victory Sanu-Goodness (13)

Listen!

Em
You think this song I've wrote is about you?
C   Em
But you're so vain, you probably think it is
Am   Em
So forget yourself just once
G
Cos this stuff is important too

Pre-chorus

C   Em   G
So listen to what I have to say

Chorus

D
The world is starving, but you don't care
Am
So can you listen now?
C   D
No, you're too busy, still doing your hair!
G   C
Your vanity really annoys me
Am   C
There are more important things than yourself!

Bethany O'Shea (12)

Writing This Song

When I'm all on my own, I think about the people that I meet
And I remember this guy, I met staring at his feet
I said, 'Man, why you looking down, so sad?'
He said, 'Girl, they hurt my feelings so bad.'
All he wanted to do was make some friends
But all they did was tease no end
So I decided to remind him . . .

It ain't about the colour of your face
It ain't about your gender or race
Wouldn't the world be better if we all got along?
That's the reason I'm writing this song.

Later on that week
I met a girl who thought I was a freak
She was all by herself
Living in a world full of wealth
She was walking down the street
But I knew that she felt incomplete
So I decided to remind her . . .

It ain't about the colour of your face
It ain't about your gender or race
Wouldn't the world be better if we all got along?
That's the reason I'm writing this song.

The reason I'm writing this song (this song)
Think about that guy
Think about that girl
Think about what's happening to the world (this world)
Ain't it sad? (makes me sad)
Society's so bad (so bad)
Reason I'm writing this song (this song).

Ellie Rice (13)

Stereotype

Some people are rich, some people are poor
Some people are cool, some people are bores
Some people are smart, some people are thick
When you're given a label, it will stick.

Popular
Is this really what you are?
Many of us are stereotypes
Unfair and skin-deep, is this right?

Some people are rich, some people are poor
Some people are cool, some people are bores
Some people are smart, some people are thick
When you're given a label, it will stick.

Forget about loving and giving
How much do you earn for a living?
Material goods, show what you are
Different classes stay very far.

Some people are rich, some people are poor
Some people are cool, some people are bores
Some people are smart, some people are thick
When you're given a label, it will stick.

Can we break out of this mould?
To me it's getting ugly and cold
Let's see people for who they really are
Not for their clothes, houses or cars.

Some people are rich, some people are poor
Some people are cool, some people are bores
Some people are smart, some people are thick
Break out of your stereotypes, it's just a trick.

Jonathan Young (16)

The Three Piggy's

The mum says goodbye
She hates them to go
She lets out a big sigh
They start to walk real slow

They meet a man
He sells lots of goods
The three pigs have a plan
They follow him to the woods

The man stood still, thrilled
The first pig saw . . .
He wants to build
A house out of straw

The second pig gets an idea
A house for him out of wood
With furniture from Ikea
His house would be very good

After eating two pigs BB was stuffed
He saw a third house and looked through the door
To see a third pig looking at his shoes that were scuffed
He could tell his belly had room for one more

He blew and he blew
The house of bricks would not fall down
The third pig laughed and said, 'Ha ha to you!'
BB Wolf stood still with a frown

He jumped on the roof
out of the chimney came something hot
The third pig saw BB and said, 'Get down you goof!'
With that BB fell screaming into a water boiling pot!

Tyler-Megan Barnett (12)

How Can It Be That I'm Still In Love With You?

My heart is in true love
But my head's in overdrive
Cos I just don't understand
Why I'm in love with you
That's right, it's you.

When I see your eyes
It puts my heart on fire
But then one touch
And I remember you're the liar.

You stole away my heart one day
But then you put it back
You broke it up so suddenly
I truly felt the whack.

You cheated and you lied
Then you left me all alone
Now you want me back
But for some reason I can't moan.

It's the weirdest thing
I can't say no to you
But then I realise
That he loves me too.

But I think our love
Is the most I'm gonna get
Cos you're all I want
You're the first I ever met.

I choose you!

Jessica Deacon (12)

Untitled

I am walking down the street
People don't usually see me coming
I wanna sing to that main beat
But what's the point if no one is listening, yeah?
I wanna be noticed
I want people to scream my name
I wanna be famous
I wanna live without my shame
I wanna be noticed
I am crushing on a guy
I don't think he even knows me
So my fame has to reach the sky
For people to see me yeah
I wanna be noticed
I want people to scream my name
I wanna be famous
I wanna live without my shame
I wanna be noticed
But could I really be this way?
Would I fit in, in our today?
My looks won't probably be perfect
And my style, well I don't have a clue
But that just won't matter when I'm singing for you
Singing songs for you
I wanna be noticed
I want people to scream my name
I wanna be famous
I wanna live without my shame
I wanna be noticed
Yeah, I wanna be noticed.

Chelsea Turner (13)

Promise Me

You left me standing here on my own,
I don't know how to get home,
I can't sleep at night,
I just got to fight,
You left me crying, dying inside,
Which is something I can't hide,
So promise me, promise me,
You'll never do this again,
Promise me, promise me,
You'll never leave me again,
Because I can't live without you.
Everything I did to help you
And everything you did to get me through,
Everything we did together,
In all different kinds of weather,
Now I'm nothing but a mess
And you like me less and less
And it's killing me.
You left me crying, dying inside,
Which is something I can't hide,
So promise me, promise me,
You'll never do this again,
Promise me, promise me,
You'll never leave me again,
Because I can't live without you.
I'll go and get hit by a lorry,
If it shows you how much I'm sorry,
Please just forgive me,
Forgive me for what I've done
And promise me!

Victoria Ankin (14)

Fear, Love And Expectation

I don't fit into society
My fingers are tied up with string
Writing upon a plane of misery
Flying a kite so far up high
Bend backwards to see
Through my eye, I'll never get caught
But I'll never get through
My heart is stopped, I'm drowned in you
Unlike him, unlike her, stuck like glue
Punishment ranged from this to that
You might pet me, you might pet my cat
Why do you have to-break-me?
Who am I? Do I know? What I need
Soaked up the greed, over seed
I'm too full up overindulged the feed
Lying upside-down, worship the ground
See me off with a metal man frown
The easy vulnerable minds
Sad and lonely sometimes
Form a band, form a group
Form an elastic loop
Buy the attitude and buy the look
Majority of us have a limited view
Use scapegoats to vent anger and blame
When the air we all breathe is the same
Focus on the bigger picture for once
The boogieman won't have you for lunch
All in all when you're faced with a wall
Try a smile, start to laugh
Makes the world's state of mind not so naff . . .

Rose Grounds (16)

Feather Heart

You hold me tight when I am down,
You make me laugh whenever I frown.
You always draw the smile on my face
And no matter what time of day
No matter how many clouds are grey,
I'd stay with you wherever the place.
You had to cry alone at night,
No one there to shine the light,
I should have been there, with you where I belong.
I wish I was there to hold your hand,
I would smile and understand,
Talk it through until all that pain had gone.
Cos that other girl,
She broke your heart,
Now it's lost and lonely,
Torn apart.
But somewhere there you saw a familiar face,
Tellin' me you loved me so,
Gave my spirit another blow,
But deep inside my feather heart, it glowed.
Feather hearted for you.
Hold on tight,
This feeling's true,
Follow your heart and you'll know what to do.
Feathered heart for you.
He's been waiting for this day,
All alone, so make his dreams come true.
Feather heart, Feather heart,
Feather heart,
Feather hearted for you.

Leah Watts (14)

Disaster

I'm stranded in my room
No one's coming in
I try to cry for help
But they ain't hearing it
My body's paralysed
I ain't got no time
Why did this happen to me?
Tell me why
Is it karma?
Have I lost my body armour
In this war of life
We are living in?
Disaster, disaster
You can't escape it even though you're running so fast
You try to scream and shout
But nothing's coming out
You better watch out for
Disaster, disaster
Drugs and violence
Are mini disasters too
To conflict on the world
Torment me and you
It leads to stabbings and crime
Sometime down the line
So I just hide in my room
Hoping that they don't find me
But i'ts not all bad
Be free and have fun
Just live your life
Don't do what I have done!

Faye McCue (12)

Untitled

Knife crime is getting worse each day
A boy got stabbed on the news called Jay
He wasn't doing anything wrong, just minding his business
The boy who did it got away without a witness
There was no way his life should have ended that night
And to any mother it would give them a big fright
They interviewed his mother to see how she was feeling
About her little Jay's life who got taken that evening
She was emotional but finally she said
She wished that her beloved Jay was still alive not dead
And she would do anything to see him again
But he was gone forever, no need to pretend
That's all she had to say but Jay was still in her heart
That cold, dark night had torn her life apart
Six weeks later the police had found a weapon
Still with the blood of Jay on it who was up in Heaven
It also had fingerprints and they linked it to a kid
A young boy named Dave who had not realised what he did
He told the police his side of the story
he said, 'I told him to stop but he just ignored me.'
Dave was trying to say that he started it first
But him stabbing Jay was much, much worse
And at such a young age he was put behind bars
And when he came out he was full of cuts and scars
Years of his life wasted, sitting in a cell
For taking Jay's life Dave felt cold as well
He felt cold in his heart, he was a cold person
His life couldn't get better it could only worsen
With no money, no house because of the life he took
This isn't the happy ending that you read in a story book.

Paul Constable (14)

Finding Us

Peeling back the fallen years,
All that damage done by beer.
Erasing angst and anarchy,
Our sharp tongues and profanity.
You take away my petty rules,
My self-help books, 'How to be Cool'.
I evict your weak façade
You put on when you're with the lads -
Of dirty jokes and filthy smiles -
We're walking long-forgotten miles
We walked when we were innocent,
When we said just what we meant.
Back when I was fine with food,
Ate it cos it tasted good.
When girls and boys were friends-no more-
We're going back to find our core,
Where nobody's afraid of us,
Where we don't confuse love with lust.
We're ripping out our fired-up views,
To let in light and banish blues.
We take these posters off our walls
To let wind whisper through the halls.
I want to know just who you are
Beyond the school and noodle bar.
At last, you get a glimpse of me,
Not just the star I want to be.
We're finding how we really feel,
Peeling backs to see what's real.
Peeling back the fallen years,
Hoping that we'll find us here.

Rebecca Grant (15)

I Miss You

I miss you,
I miss your smile
And I still shed a tear,
Every once in a while
And even though you're not here now,
You're still here somehow,
I didn't want you to go,
So I want you to know,
I miss you.
Whenever I needed you,
You came along,
You held my hand,
You kept me strong.
You were a real little friend,
We shared so many good times,
I never wanted the fun to end.
Then one day,
The horror came,
Cancer had come
And took you away.
And now I miss you, I miss your smile
And I still shed a tear
Everyone once in a while
And even though it's different now,
It's the same somehow,
My heart won't let you go,
I just want to let you know
I miss you,
Sha la la la la
I miss you!

Jessica Elderfield (14)

A Little Bit Of Music

You gotta listen to these words of advice
You might need to use it more than twice
You gotta let music take over your soul
And then you'll achieve your goals
It'll make you whole
A little bit of music will make us one
A little bit of music for everyone
A little bit of music good for the heart
It'll never ever tear you apart
If you're feeling quite down low
Why not turn on the radio?
Let the tunes take you away
You gotta listen to what I say
Don't walk away
A little bit of music opens doors
A little bit of music stops the wars
Stop world hunger, help the poor
And they won't be suffering anymore
Don't spend all day inside
Grab a guitar and head outside
Play your heart out - spread the love
Feel the power from above
So give the love
Give a little music to the world
Give a little music to break the mould
Give a little music to speed the love
Enough is never enough
A little bit of music will make us whole
A little bit of love for everyone
So have some fun.

Miles Staplehurst (13)

The Real Me

The real me
Is it really worth trying?
Will I ever get through?
When I say that I love you
Will you believe it's true?
What's the point of hiding
When you don't even know
The real me?
I don't understand
Why when you hold my hand
That you don't want to show the world
The real me
Underneath the masks
Underneath the lies
I can see
All that you really are
I don't wanna hear
And I don't wanna see
The real me
Underneath the make-up
I don't see why
You really need to hide
The real me
What's the point of me trying
When you clearly can't see
The real me standing there
When you hold my hand
I don't understand
Why you don't wanna see
The real me!

Phoebe White (13)

Baby I Love You

Dear Honeybun
I need you like the sunny sun
I love you more than money mon'
Honey I want you
Baby I love you
Baby I need you
Baby I want you
So Baby why can't I have you?
I dream of you at night
Cuddle your picture in the light
I will fight for your love to me
Until you're mine
Baby I love you
Baby I need you
Baby I want you
So Baby why can't I have you?
Your heart is what I want
My wish is to have your love
I need you more than ever
So please hear me when I say
Baby I love you
Baby I need you
Baby I want you
So Baby why can't I have you?
Dear Honeybun
I need you like the sunny sun
I love you more than money mon'
Honey, I want you
Baby I love you, I need you, I want you . . .
So why not let me have you?

Charlie Shute (14)

Love Is . . .

Love is something you can't quite explain,
Magical, spectacular, kisses in the rain,
Love is a feeling you can't stop at all,
They will make you smile and pick you up when you fall,
Love is a stare just a little too long,
An emotion that makes you feel you belong,
Love is tricky, but you can make it work if you try,
There is a shoulder to cry on, you'll never say goodbye,
Love is the main emotion which you contain,
Sacrifices and honesty, it messes with your brain,
Love is never wanting to ever be apart,
You can realise it's love right from the start,
Love is a cuddle on a cold winter's night,
Making you feel wanted and special and right,
Love is amazing but can be complicated and tough,
But the time you have with them you just can't get enough,
Love is when they will stand right by you,
Be understanding and loyal too,
Love is when you wouldn't change them for anything,
Your heart feels warm and makes you want to sing,
Love is a feeling you simply can't avoid,
If true love was to die, your heart would feel destroyed,
Love is when they help see your problems through,
It feels so magical, they make all your dreams come true,
Love is something you can't escape from,
It lets you know you need that special someone,
Love is an emotion deep down, far inside,
It is lying there in your heart with pride,
Love is an emotion locked up safe with a key,
It will be with you always, for eternity.

Stephanie Louise Heyes (14)

Lyric Potion

Lying in my bed,
Thinking in my head,
Where are the lyrics gone?
I need to make a song.
I stop and turn around,
As I hear a *f-u-n-k-y* sound.
Looking for the lyrics,
Deep inside my heart,
I don't know what to do,
Because I'm tearing apart.
The stars, sea, the ocean,
I'll make a secret potion
Made out of *lyrics!*
Find some words to put inside,
I'll find some *lyrics!*
My friends will help because they're kind,
I need some lyrics,
I burst the bubble,
I must be mad,
To think what I thought,
People think I'm sad,
What am I doing?
I think I'm crazy.
I'll start up fresh,
And pick a daisy.
I need some *lyrics!*
I know they're lurking deep inside.
I need some *lyrics!*
I've been writing them all this time,
I laugh and I sigh.

Anne O'Neill (12)

Failed

I never promised it would be OK
I didn't think it would turn out that way
One minute you're here, the next you're away
Your black clouds have took the sun's shining ray
I'm stuck in the middle with no way out
There's nothing left to do but scream and shout
I've never cried like I've cried over you
When you turn away all the stars go blue
You don't get it but I really loved you
But apparently we're rubber and glue
The past few nights I've only cried and wailed
The emptiness that I have really failed
I can't eat or drink or fall asleep
I'm just sitting her weep after weep
And every day my alarm just goes beep, beep
Your deep blue eyes in my mind I will keep
But I saw you in town with that other girl
The look on your face made me want to hurl
I've never cried like I've cried over you
When you turn away all the stars go blue
You don't get it but I really loved you
But apparently we're rubber and glue
The past few nights I've only cried and wailed
The emptiness that I have really failed
How many more days must I suffocate?
Each day it's just getting more and more late
In my whole life I've never really failed
It's not fair that I'm the one who wailed
I can't move on, I need you in my life
I loved you, I would have been a great wife!

Courtney Jayne Duckworth (14)

Painted Waters

Over these painted waters
I can hear just the faintest chorus
If I close my eyes and open my soul
I can hear a whisper talking
It's telling me to be patient
Keep faithful, know what's important
And as I fall asleep at night
I'm smiling, I feel an angel calling
It's amazing . . . that feeling
I'm shaking, my heart is beating
I keep saying it's more than dreaming
I can feel it inside me screaming
Now if I can just fight these demons
I could maybe make this moment
Last a little bit longer, honestly
It's all I have and the time is stolen
But then I look to the sand in the timer
Glance at the man in the mirror
Dream in my eyes of a hero
Everything gets just a little colder
And the temperature's below zero
And I'm waiting up for this hero
And I've never been so damn scared
I never felt this good in years
Walking over painted waters
Trying to find my way back home
Struggling through an awkward current
Heading to those fields of gold
Can you see it in my eyes? I wonder
Hoping the tide won't pull me under.

Kieran Vyas (17)

Drowning In The Pain

It's hunting me down
How can I run?
The battle is lost
Death has already won
Drowning in the pain
Suffocating in the sadness
How can I live
When this world is filled with badness?
Each day I go through
It's one step towards the end
Is there no way to know
What's around the next bend?
Being torn at the seams
By the pain in my heart
Can't go for my dreams
When I'm being torn apart
Drowning in the pain
Suffocating in the sadness
How can I live
When my world is filled with badness?
It's hunting me down
How can I run?
The battle is lost
Death has already won
Because I'm drowning in the pain
Suffocating in the sadness
How can I live
When this world is filled with badness?
The world is filled with badness
Filled with badness.

Arnold McCullough (13)

Music

I'm here today to tell a story,
About all my hopes and glory,
My love for music and rap,
On goes my baseball cap,
Hearing the beat, feeling the base,
Tapping my finger on my case,
Kids today like violence and drugs
In my eyes they're all mugs,
What your parents say is cool,
If you don't listen, you're a fool,
They will set you on the right path,
So you can sit back and laugh,
These days all the kids know,
One day I'll steal the show,
On stage giving it my all,
Not spraying the street wall,
Living my life to the full,
Guns and knives are just bull,
School is good for your brain,
Not drugs, you'll go insane,
Try your best in your life,
Don't be a loser holding a knife,
Love your family, don't be a nut,
You'll just get yourself in a rut,
So sit back and open your ears,
Wipe up them silly tears,
Work at school, you know it's right,
Your future can be bright,
You don't need trouble and strife,
If I was you I'd live life.

Daniel Roberts (14)

Love

Love is like a bubble
Pulling till they meet
When you're down
Love makes you feel
Stronger but it may
Last for longer
Love is like a tree
Growing stronger every day
Love is like a dream
You don't know where
You are, even when
You're stuck, a little
Someone knows
Love is like the
Weather, you can
Estimate but not
Be sure
Love is like the sea
Pulling and pushing together
Sometimes it's hard
But you know in
Your mind, someone's
On your side
Love is like an ocean
Starts small then grows
However far away
From home you are
You will always be
Loved.

Rachel Stirr (12)

That's It!

I saw it
I loved it
I wanted it
and if it's not real
I'll invent it
I have my obsessions
and determinations
but nothing can beat this
I saw it
I loved it
I wanted it
and if it's not real
I'll invent it
I want to be free
and live in harmony
but nothing can beat this
I saw it
I loved it
I wanted it
and if it's not real
I'll invent it
for the good, for the evil
but nothing can beat this
I saw it
I loved it
I wanted it
and if it's not real
I'll invent it
I'll invent it.

Caitlin Sweeney (12)

Through The Statue's Eye

In the time when Hayles blaze,
Overshadowed the star's lament,
We were - were we not,
This world's greatest event?
That a stone-heart like me,
Should reach out to the black,
And pull from the murk,
An eternal lover back,
Is no miracle,
Is no sin
But fate! The mighty matchmaker
The man named Chaos his so-called twin.
He announced to me his name,
'I am the lonely night,
My crime? An act of passion,
The theft of the lady's light.'
Then a promise he would whisper,
Words catching in the rain,
'I shall return my golden bounty hence
and ease the lady's pain.'

Holly May Dixon (16)

In The Sand

Walk with me
Hold my hand
I see your footprints
In the sand.

The light is dying
We're alive
This is the only place
Time we can survive.

Lauren Kerbyson (17)

I Am

I am the bullet that the gun refused
Never used but helped to abuse
I'm bulletproof, so I keep them confused
Held at gun-point by society
But they require me, so they hire me
As the stereotype in their mind
Then they fire me, so I look to the sky to try and see
The ability, to change this so called perfect world
I am a living girl, but my emotions are dead
So I write a real verse and my identity's fed
I'm hunted by hungry eyes on the streets of fear
But instead I starve them with my human tears
So they take cover while my eyes rain
The media feeds them, then they feast on my pain
Look at my face; you think you k now me, supposedly
Since you do, I'll ask you what I intend to be
A baby-making, drug-taking, knife-drilling fiend
I'm a college-going, future-growing, anti-killing teen
I am the future, and I've got my mind right
I'm everything you want . . . but your stereotype!

Michelle Murei (16)

I'll Be There

Call me when you're in the rain
Call me if you're a million miles away
Call me if you wanna see me, cos I'll be there
Just remember to call if ya need me babe
Just call me baby right way
Cos if you're there I won't have a sec to spare
Baby you know, yeah you know
I'll be there.

Jade Gullidge (11)

Celebrities

Celebs, everyone knows their names
But do they really deserve the fame?
Drinking, drugs, 'Man you're so cool'
Nah really, he's just a fool
Mouthing off to the cops
They ain't really on tops
I like movies, music! Yeah! I like them a ton
But don't you think they have too much fun?
Role models they are supposed to be
But off they go swimming in the sea
Sun, sand, a glorious pad
But everyone knows it's just a fad
There's nothing wrong with a great time
Don't wanna do the time, don't do the crime
Pull up your socks and tie your laces
Because otherwise you can't run the races
And we will put you through your paces
So put your sunglasses back in their cases
It's over now, this is your all time low
Sorry did we interrupt your flow?

David Rees (14)

Bestest Friend Of All

Oh when you're down and feeling blue
Or when you've just woken from a trance
Just remember I'll be here for you until the end of time
I'll be with you if you're up or down
'Cause you know I'm your bestest friend
Oh yes I'll be here, yes always here
I'll be here if you're feeling upset
'Cause I'm your best, your best, your bestest friend of all.

Ashley Donaghy (13)

Why Do I Still Love You?

Is it you?
Is it me
Or has this dream just become reality?
Is this life we're leading
The truth, or is it a lie?
Is this life we're living
Real, or am I still dreaming?
It must be a lie
Oh, it must be a lie . . .
Because every day I wake up
And all you do is make me cry!
How could you do this to me?
How could you make my life
Such a misery . . .
When, all that I do,
Is give you everything you ask for?
I must still be dreaming baby.
Oh yeah . . .
I must still be dreaming.
All you do is leave me . . .
Crying, and don't forget screaming!
I'm left in tears, my throat closed up.
I feel so dizzy, I can't stand up.
My head's a mess and I just,
Can't keep control . . .
Oh how . . .
Can I still love you baby?
Oh why . . .
Do I still love you?

Charlotte Murray (14)

Fantasy

People don't know me,
And they never will.
I made my own decision,
Please stop questioning me.
I don't need you,
Or anyone.
I have this fantasy,
To keep away reality.
No more questions please,
No, no more from you.
Just leave me and my fantasy,
In this fantasy.
It's illegal to be me
Cos I'm the baddest baddy
In superhero history,
Have you not seen my fantasy.
I'm the biggest mystery,
In British history.
Don't try to change me,
I want to stay this way
Cos I made myself the way I am today,
I am evil in my own way.
This is what I choose,
To be in this fantasy,
For evermore, ore, ore,
I'm now away from reality.
For the rest of my life,
But I've just found out,
It's better to be at home.

Jessica Jarvis (13)

Phoenix Never Fades

Forever and after,
We will never be forgotten . . .
For so long these days have bled into nights,
So many times when you have lifted me high.
I'm tired of this emptiness you left behind,
But I will not let it be too late this time.
This is for all you've done.
As for what I've become,
You created the man I am.
In honour I will sing:
This everlasting . . .
I will surrender my heart,
And even if you depart,
From this day forth,
For evermore,
I'll love you 'til the end.
This task ahead of me is so daunting.
I will only ever do right by your name.
No regrets left in my head,
I will not put you to shame.
This is a new page for us to write what we will;
Let's make the embers of our love burn this quill.
In honour I will sing,
From you there is no escaping . . .
I will surrender my heart,
And even if you depart,
From this day forth,
For evermore,
I'll love you 'til the end.

Matt McKay (19)

Goodbye

As I hold you
and I think through
the past, and at last I see
myself as a devotee
where I hold you - full of emotion
and honest devotion,
I can't breathe or believe
just see - you and me,
Put your trust in me, and you'll see
how my love and care
will be generously shared,
Only your eyes
make me fly - into the sky
but they save me from dying,
I'll show you a place
where the stars shine with glitter
and the moon shimmers,
Just watching your face
forces me to embrace
you closer to my soul,
Now I know I've reached my goal
we just be
as time ticks
and I drift to a close
and awake from the overdose
doing anything with you
helps me make it through,
Do I have to?
Yes I do - say goodbye . . .

Haya Mulhem (12)

Fading Heartstrings

Once when the sun lit the sky,
We walked together hand in hand,
These memories of you will last a lifetime,
But as the sun sets on this barren land,
We had to let go and find our own way,
Losing you,
Was the one thing that never crossed my mind,
I never thought,
The day would come where I was left behind,
That sun soon faded to grey,
And my heartstrings pulled like you'd turned me away,
At first I didn't understand why you had to go,
And time will never heal these wounds,
But now I can see and I finally know,
Why you were taken away,
I cannot control this thing called time,
But know this wherever you are,
This heart still remembers,
No matter where and no matter how far,
I will always remember your heart,
And this thing called death I lost you to,
Could never make me leave you,
Now that the sun is gone and the stars are here,
That loneliness might creep,
But still I know you're near,
I can feel those eyes watching over me,
Seeing all I see,
I'll find you again someway,
Some way.

Jade Tomlins (15)

What If?

He was my best friend, he loved me till the end
He hated seeing me with anyone else
He liked how I did my hair, he loved my sexy sultry stare
He wanted to be my only one
I was too blonde to see, too close minded to look in front of me
Why couldn't I see, see he was stood there offering his love,
See he wanted to save my heart, not tear it apart?
These are the things that I regret
Now I can't stop myself from thinking:
'What if that was different?' What if?
He drove me where I needed, he bought me all I had seen and
He saved me every time, he sat with me when I cried
He backed me up when I lied, but I was blind
I was so stupid, where were you, baby Cupid?
Why couldn't I see, see he was stood there offering his love,
See he wanted to save my heart, not tear it apart?
These are the things that I regret
Now I can't stop myself thinking:
'What if that was different?' What if?
I am sorry, I was so blind
All of this worry and you should've been mine
Why couldn't I see, see he was stood there offering his love,
See he wanted to save my heart, not tear it apart?
These are the things that I regret
Now I can't stop myself thinking:
'What if that was different?' What if?
What if, if I loved you?
What if, if there were something I could do?
What if it were different? What if?

Rebecca Wyatt (14)

999

Call 999, my heart is breaking
Left to bleed, it's bruised and aching
What ya done to me I can't understand
I'm never gonna trust another man.

Why did you leave me, why did you go?
Tell me darlin', I have to know
Did she steal your heart, had you had enough?
Tell me darlin', had I run out of love?
When I used to think of you
I didn't know what to do
'But darlin',' I said, 'my heart is tender.'
When I looked in your eyes
I was hypnotised
Well honey, you were the great pretender!
Take me to A&E
This ain't no accident but emergency
Somebody can you help me please?
Oh doctor, can you see
This aching heart is breaking me?
Give me some cures or remedies
All these sleepless nights, bags under my eyes
There's no disguise, I'm not OK
Singing on my guitar, wonderin' where on Earth you are
You're so, so far away.

Call 999, my heart is breaking
Left to bleed, it's bruised and aching
What ya done to me I can't understand
I'm never gonna trust another man.

Caris Twyman (12)

The Light Will Help Me Breathe

Life's dark, I cannot see the way
Darkness is creeping up on me
Ripping the air from my lungs
And I'm finding it hard to breathe
My life restarts today
I'm gonna find a path to my destiny
I know I'll find it somewhere, out there

The light's out of sight
I'm getting too weak to fight
I can't stay awake
My eyes keep closing and
I need a new road to take
Feeling sick when I step out of place
I still hold the memory of your face
In my mind it's fading, quickly fading

We used to be so happy
Look now, we're falling apart
But you get to live the rest of your life
We used to be so happy
You know we're falling apart
Though you get to live the rest of your life
You're still so sad, so sad

There's got to be light here somewhere
I need it to help me breathe
I know the light, it's out there
I think I've seen it before
I know I've seen it before, somewhere.

Rebecca Ingram-Jones (15)

Don't Change

Some days I wonder why
I'm different from the crowd
Why my eyes are tiny
Why my hair sticks out?

But someone told me
Don't change
Just to be the same
And if you do
You should be ashamed

Some days I feel an outcast
Like I don't belong
But I'll be rejected
If I don't play along

But someone told me
Don't change
Just to be the same
Ad if you do
You should be ashamed

But one day I'll realise
That I'm someone special
And shouldn't compromise

'Cause someone told me
Don't change
Just to be the same
And if you do
You should be ashamed.

Mishelle Waqasi (15)

Cross Roads

Split in two, I don't know where to go
Something tells me I should know
But I don't, I don't, I don't, I don't know
Two paths, two tracks
Which do I use?
Two lives, two futures
Which do I choose?
Decisions, decisions, decisions,
Decisions, choices, I don't know how to make it
I don't know which heart I'm breakin'
I don't know where to go, I'm stuck
Standing at the cross roads
Waiting for it to come to me
Will I have them begging on their knees?
Please don't do that, please don't, please!
I just can't take it anymore
I wanna go back right to the start
I wanna start over, start over again
And make sure this never happens
Two paths, two tracks
Which one do I use?
Two lives, two futures
Which do I choose?
Decisions, decisions, decisions,
Decisions, choices
I wanna go back right to the start
I wanna start over, start over again
And make sure this never happens again.

Lydia McCarthy (13)

Street Beat

No matter where you look
The whole world around
Different kinds of kids
Make different kind of sounds
Some use their hands
Some use their feet
To make a little rhythm
To make a little beat
Street beat, street beat
Everybody knows a street beat
In the playground
After school
Here's a beat
That's really cool
When everybody does it
It comes alive
So come on, join in
Do the hand jive
And tin-can kids
Street beat, street beat
Everybody knows a street beat
Well by now, you know
Street beats are hot
And there's no doubt
A catchy rhythm
A catchy song
Will travel the
Whole wide world around.

Nisha Ahmed (14)

Fame Is The Name Of The Game

Walking down the road of shame
I wish I knew all this before I came to fame
Cos now I'm asking myself if I would do it again
Is all this money worth the grief and pain?
Not even love can get me through the day
I'm sure I would have it another way.
Cos love is like a fast-paced train
Or a never-ending hurricane
My world has been taken from under my feet
I'm wondering if I should just admit defeat
Why did all the good perks have to stop?
I'm lying low now cos I've been brought down from the top
Not even love can get me through the day
I'm sure I would have it another way
Cos love is like a fast-paced train
Or a never-ending hurricane.
Life is not as easy as those singers make out
Step out of line and you'll be on the cover of SHOUT!
Why can't the press see that I'm just the same as you?
I don't know how to show them, what should I do?
Not even love can get me through the day
I'm sure I would have it another way
Cos love is like a fast-paced train
Or a never-ending hurricane
Through this I found out who my true friends are
They don't care if I'm zero, hero or a star
I used to dream of fans following me here and there
But now that I'm famous I no longer care.

Paige Lauren Izquierdo (12)

Down On The Ice Now

I came around the corner
I saw you and her
I said, 'What the heck are you doing?'
You couldn't give me an answer
'This isn't what it looks like,'
You said that to me
Don't take me for a fool
Can't believe I couldn't see
My heart was glowing
But now it's going
It's burning, burning out
You begged me not to go,
'Do you love me?'
I said, 'No.'
Hear this now
Baby, when you slip
It's like falling over ice skating
And I can't get myself off the ground
And baby, when you slip
It's like my heart suddenly stops
And I can't breathe
So take me again
Baby, when you trip
It's like I'm slipping on the ice rink
I wonder will you help me out?
I'm down on the ice rink now
Why'd you let me fall?
I thought I had it all.

Shelby Lucier (12)

The World To Me

Waking up on a Saturday morning,
climbing out of bed, but I'm still yawning,
takes ten minutes to do my hair and make-up.
Still grieving about the night of our break-up.
I go downstairs to get some breakfast,
I don't really care what I eat,
I'm going out to town this morning, 'cause
me and best friends are going to meet,
I can't believe how selfish it is of you,
to ignore the pain that I've been going through
and I don't know how much more I can take,
with all the decisions and sacrifices I've had to make,
but I trusted you with the things I said,
not known what's in your head.
Now you're with that other girl can't you see,
you are the world to me?
Stepping out onto the busy street,
to catch my bus, the X13, with my lipstick, jacket
and high heels up upon my feet.
The bus stops at the city centre,
so I can meet my friends in Coffee #1.
Take a look at the door and guess who enters?
You with your new girl, what's her name?
I hope you begin to share my pain
as you take a look around and glance my way,
realising that I cannot stay,
as I walk past you, you stop me
and say, 'Can't you see, you are the world to me?'

Harriette Cooke (15)

Love Struck

Never give up, if you still want to try
Never wipe your tears, if you still want to cry
Never settle for the answer, if you still want to know
Never say you don't love him, if you can't let him go.
When life gets rough
And when people put you down
Show the world your beautiful smile
And hide away that frown
Don't fear something you've never felt before
Don't think it's wrong to go and ask for more
Don't let other people stop you having fun
Don't be too serious when life has just begun
When life gets rough
And when people put you down
Show the world your beautiful smile
And hide away that frown
Want mistakes to stay in the past?
Want the memories that seem to last?
Want the days to be much longer?
Want our love to become much stronger?
When life gets rough
And when people put you down
Show the world your beautiful smile
And hide away that frown
Give as much as you expect back
Give respect which others might lack
Give a smile when the sun shines above
Give affection and *bang*, you found love.

Rebecca Booth (15)

How It Was

Remembering all the times gone by
The laughs, the jokes, no reason why
I did the things I shouldn't do
And now I turn and look at you
My mind's a blur with what we've done
Mum and Dad were my number one
With my sister we have done a lot
We have laughed and cried and maybe not
Said the things we should have said
But always sorted out for bed
The holidays that we've been on
The sun, sea and friends that's gone
Mum and Dad work hard all year
So that me and Lauren get Christmas cheer
We never have to ask them twice
Mum and Dad are very nice
At school, I do my very best
But sometimes I can be a pest
On the weekend we both play our sport
Rugby for me, gym for Lauren
And a headache for Mum and Dad to sort
I feel like time is moving on
And worry about when they are gone
But then they sit and say to me
That people don't just go away
They stay beside us, all our days
For all the people yet to come
And keep the future moving on.

Nathan Harrop (12)

I Need This Rhythm

Yes, I am the lyrical genius
I write the hits, trust me I'm serious
I need some time
Let me put my pen to paper
Cos if I don't, I'll just forget later
With every word that flows from mind to hand
There's a feeling
You won't understand
I need this rhythm
Cos this right here, this is my time
I'm sick of the way
This world likes to hurt
I'm only 13
And I already know how it works
Just give me that one chance, hey
You need to feel what I'm trying to say
Cos if you don't listen to me now
Then I'm honestly and truly about to bow out
Seriously, if there's anyone else
That can make you feel this way
Then go on, go ahead just say
And with this feeling you don't understand
Making the flow from mind to hand
I tell you now, this is it
All I have given
Is now in this rhythm
Because this right here . . .
This is now my time!

Holly Taylor (13)

Would Daddy Even Care?

I was only young
When you left
You told me everything would be OK
But where are you today?
You used to tell me that I could be
Anything I wanted
But now I'm living in misery
You went away
And left me here alone
So tell me this

Would Daddy even care
If I went away?
Would he shed a tear
if my life came to an end?
He left me standing here alone
And now I feel like no one's home
So tell me
Would Daddy even care?

I thought you were king
In my eyes you were
Looking back at the photos
I'm finding it hard to see
What went wrong today?
I'm sat here wondering
If it was me, am I to blame?
Please tell me
Would Daddy even care?

Jasmine Bayes (14)

You And Me

The night-time room shimmers in a wine-soaked blur,
Your face above, hand outstretched, 'Come up.'
Silently, smiling, in my thin white slip, I slip
Into your bed, your chest, your arms around me.
Your nose presses my nape through swathed dark hair,
You cling me to you, charged breathing; charged air
Caressing my stomach, we tighten together,
You kiss the taut skin on my perfumed shoulder.

Comfortably we sleep, huddled together,
You cradled by the wall, half the bed left over,
The first tinny lark of the morning and we relapse,
Grasping at the shadows that recede before us,
Your hand over mine, reassuring. *I won't walk out of your life.*
My hand over yours, stroking, like it was rightfully mine,
A myriad of alarms, phones, light, my conscience,
We sit up, bare skin to bare skin, pretentiously oblivious.

We wore white the first night, pure and innocent,
Like lambs to the slaughter, brides to the altar
Before the knowledge spilling. We wore black on the last day,
The colour of grieving, nothingness, nothing left after the leaving,
Solemn and expectant, complaining in play,
We spent time frugally, went bankrupt anyway,
Surrounded by beauty - wreath of painted eggs on the fire extinguisher,
Minute, detailed, loving gestures. Our hands brushed, often,
but never curled . . .
And as we embraced I felt in you the slim health of redemption,
We smile from each other's pictures, my heart in two directions.

Rosemary Cowhig (17)

I Wish

I wish you were the one
To hold me close
And whisper in my ear
Those three words
It means so much to hear.

Chorus
Being with you is what I want
And I know it's hard but it means a lot
My heart's draining with hopes and dreams
That we'd live to be together but probably not
I love you more than words.

I wish you were the one
To lend your jacket
When I'm cold
To hold my hands
And keep me close

I wish you were the one
I could say was
Mine and smile
To kiss and cuddle
To save me from denial.

I wish you were the one
I'd kiss underneath
The Christmas tree
I'd share my Valentine's Day with you
And you'd learn to love me.

Jessica Perks (14)

Michael Jackson

It's very funny
Now that you are gone
People have the audacity to say
That they liked you all along

Now that you are not here
Your talent is appreciated a lot more
From when you were young
We knew a legend was born

Your music was fantastic
Your songs were a killer
Your energy was terrific
But mostly your album 'Thriller'

When fans went to your concert
They went mad
The way you sing and dance
The way you perform 'Bad'

You gave such energy towards the audience
When you performed 'Another Part of Me'
The music gets the beat in with the flow
You saw screaming fans say, 'Michael, look at me!'

Now that you're resting in peace
I never got a chance to say
How much I love you
And how much of a big fan I am of your music.

RIP Michael Jackson.

Tahja Ronai Adeyingbo (12)

Deviant

She takes her time, says she's fine, keeps herself to herself
But in debates with her mates, boy - she's something else
She's got a way with words, hot topics of the world

Oh, it's the voice of a new generation

Because she's deviant, unfettered, fain
Free from society's corrupt chains
The page is clean, a new book's begun
So don't tell her that she's too young

He goes with the flow, stays mellow, easy-going for all
But injustice, inane cruelty, always makes his blood boil
He wants to make a change, things will never be the same

Oh, it's the voice of a new generation

Because he's deviant, unfettered, fain
Free from society's corrupt chains
The page is clean, a new book's begun
So don't tell him that he's too young

You've gotta fight for what you believe in
You gotta speak up for what is right

Because we're deviant, unfettered, fain
Free from society's corrupt chains
The page is clean, a new book's begun
So don't tell us that we're too young

Oh deviant
Deviant.

Susan Dowell (14)

The Move

He told me he's moving
I try to hold back the tears
It's too hard, I start crying
This is the worst of my fears
All those memories we shared
Together day by day
My heart just gets torn
In each and every way.
My tears for you mean oh so much
But in time they will all lose touch
On the last day that we will share
I'll hold you close and keep you by
Cos the love I gave out is ever so rare
And to get you back all I can do is try
I told you I love you
And you know I still do
So baby don't stop crying
Because I miss you.

Chloe Mason (13)

I Still Love You

When you're looking in the mirror
Check behind
Just to see who's there
Through the deepest despair
Where all hope is lost
How you have left me
This way with
A broken heart and this fear
Of what I may become
A lonely soul deep inside
But all I know is that
I still love you.

Charlotte Simpson (13)

Out My Window

I looked out my window
And what did I see?
All of my family
How can it be?

When I dream these things
I want them to come true
Even though I don't really care
I mean too.

When I dream these things
It's not reality
It's make-believe
How can this be?
Why is it me?

Then through the crowds
I spot my true family
They do love me
How can this be?
Are they here for me?

Charlotte Baldwin (13)

The One

The walls are tearing down
The darkness fills the town
The shadow left in the clouds of the list
Is the sun hiding from the moon's raised fist?
You could - I bet you would - but you can't
You've left it for too long
Watch as the music escapes the song
Admitting the fact, the fact - you were wrong
Waitin' and waitin' and waitin' and waitin'
On the one, on the one
On the one, on the one.

Jack Radford (14)

My Music

When I hear my music
My mind starts making up a beat
My soul can't stop
Like it's gonna jump out of my feet
Turn the music up!

The music that plays
Is not just a hobby for me
Music's all I got, why can't you let me be?

The beat and the rhythm and the lyrics
That I like to write
The six strings on my back
Don't need anything but that

Nobody can take the music out of me
The beat that runs to my feet
So just leave me
And let me be

The music that plays
Is not just a hobby for me
Music's all I got, why can't you let me be?

The beat and the rhythm and the lyrics
That I live to write
The six strings on my back
Don't need anything but that
The music that plays
Is not just a hobby for me.

Toni Solly (12)

Celebs

Here's a little song about
the rich and the famous;
the stars who everyone
knows what their name is.

There's Posh with her specs,
Angelina with her lips;
There's Beyonce with her bum
and Shakira with her hips!

And don't forget Amy -
Winehouse, I mean.
The one with big hair
that really isn't clean.

And what happened to
Avril, Kate Nash
and Sandi Tom?
they just seemed to disappear -
anyone know where they've gone?

There's a lot I haven't mentioned
but if I did, it would take me years
I'd start off looking like Amanda
and end up looking like Piers!

And although they can be annoying
and let the fame go to their brain,
without all the celebs
life just wouldn't be the same!

Emily Mills (14)

Helter-Skelter

As I trundle down into the room
Three jackals howling - like *boom, boom*
This is the part that I realise
My life is hangin' onto the edge of a knife.
It can go two ways, the good, the bad, the happy, the sad
I just gotta choose
Yo, what's to lose? Not my life
Cos if I choose the right path
The night devils could get me, flip me 360
And send me on a different one.
The straight and narrow one to having a handgun
Believing I am doing good
Believing I am the modern day Robin Hood
With just one flaw
I rob from the rich but don't give to the poor.
I just keep it with myself
To expand my personal wealth
Cos it doesn't even matter how I do it
How I pursue it
As long as I get my jewels in the end.
I feel I am the better man
Well in fact I am just a wealthier man
As the grief pours down on me
Just like a monsoon
Affecting others too
But this time there's no shelter
Cos life's one big helter-skelter.

Tom Sandry (16)

I'll Be . . .

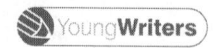

I'll be what you want me to be
Whether a lover, a friend or just plain me
No, I don't know your opinion
But baby, let me close that distance
Open your eyes and breathe
I'll be what you want me to be
Whatever you've looked for
Whatever you need
Simplicity at its best
No need to worry and stress
Let yourself go and see
You've had my soul for far too long
No I won't turn away -
It's not time to move on
You don't have to say what you feel
What we have is a done deal
If you want me, I'll be there
If you don't, then I will stay clear
It's you and me, effortlessly
You've had my soul for far too long
No, I won't turn away -
I'm holding on
You've had my soul for far too long
No, I can't turn away
I can't move on
I'll be what you want me to be
Whether a lover, a friend or just plain . . . me.

Holly Blood (14)

The Star Shines As You Love Someone

Look at me, a shining star
Going, going down to your love
Come to me, come to me
Feel a star looking down to you
Come to me, come to me
Feel a star looking down at love
Look at love, as a shining star
Come to love, come to love someone
Feel a boy kiss to you down in your heart
Come to love, come to love the whole world
Feel a boy kiss you with love
Look at the flower's shape, as a blue and white star
Flower blowing in the sunshine
Feel the flower shine back and smiling
Flower blowing in the blue sky
She sat down with her boyfriend at the seaside
They swim down to the seashore
Feel the blue-green coloured sea
Come down to the seaside
Feel as you swim in Spain
They see the seaside
Going swimming, going swimming with dolphins
The sunset going, going down in the water
Dolphins jump, jump out of shiny blue sunset-coloured water
This is the world we live in
We chose this, the world
We made this Earth.

Zoe Hunt (16)

I Don't Need You

Why can't these things ever be
The way you want them?
The way you need them
To be?
Free from everything
And everyone
I don't need
You
I don't need you.

Nothing's gonna be the same
'Til you stop
playing this love game
can't you see?
Can't you see the pain
In my eyes
When you hear me screaming?
And wonder why,
Why I cry?

I am broken now
You left me
Bleeding in the street lights
Black blood in the night,
Weeping for you
To come back
And finish me
Please.

Katy Dell (14)

Without You

The violent bang leaves this shallow house
Rattling after you
And as it slams you have it all
And all that we thought meant something to you
The darkest stair is where we sit
As our life walked out the door
Your footsteps echo down the path
Like memories, they disappear . . .

No more lying, no more crying
When enough becomes enough
No more aching, no more hating
Coarse sensation left us rough
No more trying, no more failing
As you said it's all too much
And you left us all to live
But that's fine
That's life without you

The violent words that lead his rule
Never laid a hand on us
Now they lie idle, rejected, unstable
As your hand glides away
It's just . . .
He never touched you either
Because he loved you too
Just hated the rejection
And we pity him for you.

Benjamin Cope (17)

The Ghostly Moan

The terrible sounds everywhere I go
The screeching of bats and the howling of wolves
The sound getting louder every night
All you've got to do is scream like that
See all the people frightened to death
Going away from houses to stay safe from it
The ghostly moan stuck in your head.

The ghostly moan, listen close
Coming from the country's coast
The ghostly moan, listen close
It's one of the things that scare people the most.

The horrible sound in the streets and roads
The clawing of bats
And the breathing of wolves
The sound getting closer to you all night
All you've got to do is run like that
Hear all the people crying all day
The scariest moan every day and every night
The ghostly moan aching in your mind.

The ghostly moan, listen close
Coming from the country's coast
The ghostly moan, listen close
It's one of the things that scare people the most.

The sound getting more deathly all the nights
The ghostly moan, sucking you in.

Sebastien Reece (10)

The Power

I don't need you next to me
I just wanna go home
I don't need you to hold my hand
I just wanna be alone.

Because I've got the power
This game, I have played
I've got my working hands
I've got the power
I've got the key
To unlock all the secrets
About you and me

The treasure chest awaits me
And I'm full of fear
What if you don't like me?
What if the answer's here?
I don't need anyone's help
I can do it on my own
I'm an independent girl
I don't need a clone

Oh because I've got the power
Yeah, I've got the key
To unlock all the secrets
To unlock all the secrets
About . . .
You and me!

Amy O'Meara (12)

Rain

The rain falls from the heavens above
Fills up puddles
It looks as clear as crystal
It sounds like the footsteps of a creeping robin
Pitter-patter, pitter-patter
The rainbow appears

Now the rain is fierce
Falling faster and faster
Heavier the rain gets
It soaks the people below with a wet, cold touch
A touch as cold as ice
You feel as miserable as a mouse with no food
It smells so damp like a corner of a dark and dingy prison cell

The rain turns into hailstones
Banging as they hit the ground
No longer has a sweet little pitter-patter
Thunder and lightning appears joining the heavy hailstones
Terrible feeling inside you, miserable, lonely
I would rather stay inside

The rain calms down
Fills up puddles
It looks as clear as crystal
It sounds like the footsteps of a creeping robin
Pitter-patter, pitter-patter
The rainbow appears.

Dannielle Rose (13)

A New Beginning

Every time I saw your face
My heart it lit up and it screamed
Then you walked away from me
My heart you ripped it at the seams.

You used to be my whole world
The only thing in my head
Now I've got to shut you out
When you left me I felt dead.

Now I sit here in my room
I sit alone and cry
I sit here thinking
Without you I could die.

I hope to see you again some day
Maybe when my heart's been sealed
Maybe when I've moved on
When the wounds have healed.

I just want to be myself again
For this pain to end
To be myself again
For these scars to mend.

So I'm gonna stand up, stand tall
I'm gonna forget, forgive it all
Stand up, stand tall
Forget, forgive it all.

Alanna Holdsworth (15)

Bridge Over Water

You said that everythin' was all right
Then you walked away from me into the night
I never thought I'd see that comin'
I never thought I'd lose your smile.

All of a sudden you then used me
You made me protect from the rough rocks and sea
I never thought my heart would break
I never thought I'd helped you for your sake.

Well, I will never be your bridge over water
Just to keep yourself clean and dry
No, I will never be your bridge over water
Just to love me then make me cry
Go find another place to cross
Cos this bridge is much better . . . than you think.

My time won't be wasted no more
Now, if you'll excuse me, I have to go . . .

Well, I will never be your bridge over water
Just to keep yourself clean and dry
No, I will never be your bridge over water
Just to love me then make me cry
Go find another place to cross
Cos this bridge is much better . . . than you think.

You see I will never be your bridge over water . . .
No more.

Olivia Church (13)

Time For Me

All I want is time
Time spent you and me
Let's talk and I'll be fine
Just make some time for me.

I can't stop loving
I can't stop hurting
Why can't you see
You're killing me?

One kiss, one touch
Treasured, means so much
Feels so true
Is it anything to you?

You use me and hurt me
Pick me up then drop me
I play the fool so true
I continue loving you.

I can't stop loving
I can't stop hurting
I can't stop forgiving
And it's killing me.

Loving you hurts me
Trusting you wounds me
Why can't you see
You're destroying me?

Kayleigh Tompkins (14)

Gotta Get Out

I am a nameless face, another disgrace,
I laugh, I joke, coins fall, I'm broke,
Saw him crash that Ford Fiesta, eternal siesta,
A life long boulder, heavy on my shoulder.

I make up the truth, my lips are loose,
Another strange encounter, lucky they found her,
Her hair wet with sick, a precious tulip,
Vodka burned, heads are turned.

A purple passage, I know I've got baggage,
Gotta get out of living as a teenage lout,
I want to be free, free to be me,
Game over, another year older, pride on my shoulder.

Pushed to the limit, I'm hard though innit,
Boys in blue, said they're looking for you,
Skins unravelled, whispers have travelled,
I'm on the ground, never to be found.

Game over, another year older, chip on my shoulder,
I'm an unexplained science, driven by defiance,
Just one more statistic, 'cause I went ballistic,
Got a bad deal, now I know it's for real.

A purple passage, I know I've got baggage,
Gotta get out of living as a teenage lout,
I want to be free, free to be me,
Game over, another year older, pride on my shoulder.

Jezel Jones (17)

Summer's End

Leaves are turning golden-brown
Growing old and falling down
Making the Earth a bed of fire
Now is summer's end.

Trees are losing all their glory
Going is their sunny story
Leaving arms aloft but bare
Now is summer's end.

As the colour of russet gold
Leaves the land a blanket white
The welcome warmth becomes so cold
Bringing forth our premature night.

Autumn's warm colours faded away
The nothingness seems here to stay
Smothering where once was life
Now is summer's end.

Yet through the snow upon the ground
Delicate flowers raise up proud
Showing life had never left
Never was summer's end.

Know the sun does never die
Merely takes a welcome rest
And when tis winter's turn to be
Comes summer, spring and autumn's best.

Reann Radcliffe (15)

Lucky Star

Cried my last tear for you, I will never again
Hear my heart beat for you, I refuse to feel pain
But still I know, when I stand all alone
That I can't survive without you

Cradle me in the dark, I feel you slipping away
Feel my heart crack in two and then burst into flames
But still I pray this is all just a dream
And today I will wake beside you

But I can't help but wish on my lucky star
That one day you'll return and pick me up in your car
And I will sing till my voice starts to crack
And thank my lucky star that you're back

I saw your face last night, all I dream of is you
An angel glowing bright, what a glorious view
But then I wake and crash down back to Earth
To a place where I can't be with you

Living in a lie, which I want to be true
Is it too much to ask, that I can be with you?
Memories fade and they stop coming back
I just hope that I don't forget you

But I can't help but wish on my lucky star
That one day you'll return and pick me up in your car
And I will sing, till my voice starts to crack
And thank my lucky star that you're back.

Heather King (15)

Untitled

I'm not looking for the type of words that make me want to cry
But every time I see your face I'm protected from all harm
So wrap me in your arms tonight
And write a love line on my palm
Ooh-ooh-ooh- ooh-aaaah

I think about you every day
And I see our future in my heart
And nothin' can change this perfect melody
And change it into a different harmony
That's just how strong I think our love will be if you're with me
So lock your heart into the words I am singing now
The words inside my mouth are dying to lie on your face
I looooove youuuuuu.

Taeeba Rahim (9)

Child

Lay down thy head child
Lay still and breathe
See thy sun child
See me leave
Stand thy child
Stand up for thyself
Meet those who can't child
Meet the bullies, victims and those who watch
Be somebody child
Be the one who controls themself
Inspire thy child
Inspire the world to change
Change thy child
Change for the better.

Katie Whelpton (14)

I Simply Loved You

Every step I take
Thinking of something to say to you
Not knowing if my heart's gonna break
How does it feel to know I love you?

Now I'm waiting
To know if you love me too
Although I can't change the mind of fate
Baby I hope it's not too late.

I dream of you in a place
A place that's warm and dark
But just so you know
This is a special place for your heart.

Now you break my heart
Now I see the truth
Now I know what I meant to you
Now that you've acted like a jerk.

Somewhere along the road
We went wrong
I dreamt we would have 'a song'
But you decided not to sing along.

I would've given anything for you
I even dreamt for a kiss or two
But you were poison
It's gonna be alright without you.

Hannah Garrett (13)

Breaking Out

It's the drumming beat that drives us
It's the pen on paper that tells
It's the paintbrush on the painting
That keeps us from our shells.

The music that makes it happen
The music that never ends
The song that is being written
On which our life depends.

The story always writing
The pen with endless ink
The tale that life remembered
It's gone in a blink.

The picture always changing
The painting that shows the way
Our life is never set for us
Don't waste your life away.

This you should remember
That life is too much
Always keep your head high
And keep life in a clutch.

It's breaking out that's important
To keep us from our shell
Never let your spirit dampen
'Less life is a living Hell.

Stephen Shelmerdine (15)

The Lone Traveller

My only company is in the form of vultures
Who stare at me with watchful eyes
So unforgiving as I cross the wastelands
They wait patiently for those who die.

And accompanying me on my way is a friend
Who only disappears when the night-time falls
He is someone who cannot speak at all
He cannot cry out a warning or call.

He is my shadow, there at each place I go
Synchronised steps, joined as one forever
He is the only thing I have to remind me I survive
And, though strange, we'll always be together.

Sometimes I long for someone to talk with
Perhaps even somebody to love me
And I could go home with imaginary camera in hand
To show everyone what I see.

Yet I should think in now and not always
And forget about what the future may hold
Forget about how crazy I may be going
Forget about how warm it is, yet I feel so cold.

But when the time comes and I finally die
Somebody will write what I have known
What things I've seen, smelt and heard
And that I had walked alone.

Eleanor Hynds (14)

Neon Lights

Her name fashioned from neon lights
Lit up the drab and gloomy nights,
But no better than the one before
And who's heard of her anymore?

Neon lights and cocktail drinks
You just ignore the missing links,
A pretty, cordial, party queen
Yet, in all your life, where have you been?

Even Time is tiring, it's just turned two
And I don't know what's got into you,
Partying, but alone - no longer seventeen.
Coins cascading as you reach the limousine.

Neon lights and cocktail drinks
You just ignore the missing links,
A pretty, cordial, party queen
Yet, in all your life, where have you been?

What's happened to the girl I remember
Who threw snowballs hardest in cold December?
We gave you wings and you soared so high,
But now you're crashing, crashing down.

Neon lights and cocktail drinks
You just ignore the missing links,
A pretty, cordial, party queen
Yet, in all your life, where have you been?

Melissa Gardner (16)

Music Is My Life

M ichael Jackson was the king of pop
U sher doesn't like rock
S noop Dogg loves to rap
I ndoors wearing his favourite cap
C lassical music

I s not my thing
S inging loudly you cannot win

M any people want to sing because
Y ou get to wear lots of bling

L eona Lewis has a great voice
I guess she made the right choice
F riends and families go to watch their favourite singers and
E njoy the music, singing like winners.

Kellie Williams (14)

How Can You Do This To Me?

OK, you wanna go out sometimes
Have some fun sometimes
Well, that is fine with me
But if you leave me behind
And go with someone else
How can you do this to me?
OK, you want to chillax sometimes
Have peace sometimes
Well, that is fine with me
But when I want peace
You making noise around me
How can you?
How can you do this to me?

Charlotte Elizabeth West (10)

You Say I'm Being Paranoid

I just want to tell you I don't know where to look
When you're casually singing those words
I feel eyes constantly peering at me
Each person wondering what has occurred
You say I'm being paranoid
And that I dream thoughts in my head
I can't explain how wrong you are
Now every new song you sing I dread
I will try hard to get used to
These harsh words that you sing
It just hurts to hear the word 'I'
Even though it's not to do with 'us'
Or remotely anything
You say I'm being paranoid
And that I dream thoughts in my head
I can't explain how wrong you are
Now every new song you sing I dread
I did not choose to fall in love
With a man of which music is his soul
I've coped for three years and more
But wondering if my heart will always
Remain whole
you say I'm being paranoid
And that I dream thoughts in my head
I can't explain how wrong you are
Now every song you sing I dread.

Alexandra Pointer (19)

Me And You

I'm sitting here, alone in my room, thinking 'bout the past.
Wonderin' whatever happened between us.
You know how I'm feelin' right now, you know I love you
And I know that there's never gonna be another me and you.
I'm just talking to you on MSN, waiting for a reply.
Hoping that when the convo goes orange it'll say I love you.
But no that's just another stupid dream I'm having ain't it?
And I know there's never gonna be another me and you.
Even though my friends were there, I felt so alone.
I never got why every time I had someone else,
You said, 'You can do so much better than him.'
Then when you first called me your baby it was my dream.
I always hated getting up for school just knowing you had her . . .
I just wonder why you always give me that look,
The same look you gave me when we were going out,
You made it seem like you loved me, well huh? D'you?
I'm sitting here, alone in my room, thinking 'bout the past . . .
Wonderin' whatever happened between us.
You know how I'm feelin' right now, you know I love you
And I know that there's never gonna be another me and you.
I'm just talking to you on MSN waiting for a reply.
Hoping that when the convo goes orange it'll say I love you.
But no that's just another stupid dream I'm having, ain't it?
And I know there's never gonna be another me and you.
I have just missed every kiss, every hug, I have missed everything . . .
I just wanna be safe in your arms again please . . . ?

Bethany Picton (12)

Distorted Reflection

They're drifting apart
And forming a gap,
All the colours dimming down
To grey,
It's the sky
It's the same but it's different,
Different viewpoints,
Different worlds,
It's the sky
It's the same, but it's different,
Viewpoints, worlds,
It's a distorted reflection.
It's as if the stars
Could reflect the moods
Of the million diverse faces
Below them.
It's the sky
It's the same, but it's different
Different viewpoints,
Different worlds,
It's the sky
It's the same, but it's different,
Viewpoints, worlds,
It's a distorted reflection,
It's a distorted reflection,
It's a distorted reflection.

Alice Langridge (14)

Lies

There you walk away
Leaving me angry and alone
I want to be there I need you to be okay
But as you lie
Dreams shatter before my eyes
You're helping no one
Pushing me further aside
Actions speak louder
At least that's what they say
Thought it's this raw feeling
These words, that push me away
Standing at my side
Truth yearns from inside
Damaged by the lies
This is how my pain hides
But as you lie
Dreams shatter before my eyes
You're helping no one
Just killing me inside
Cos you know
Those lies
Lead to me
You must see
You're pushing me
Killing me
Aside.

Ella Stirling (15)

Cry Out

I cry out for you in the night
Because I need you tonight to comfort me
Because I can't see
What's going to happen to me.

You say it's okay and you say,
'Close your eyes,' as you sway
And you say it's okay and you say,
'Close your eyes,' as you sway.

I cry out for you in the night
Because I need you tonight to comfort me
Because I can't see
What's going to happen to me.

You say it's okay and you say,
'Close your eyes,' as you sway.

Jasmine Blanchard (12)

Friendship's Fogging The Way

You're stood right there teasin' me,
Oblivious to the face that I could be,
The one you love, the one you need,
Oh please baby, don't make my heart bleed.
I'm sick of being only friends,
It's driving me round the bend,
Just kiss me now you crazy fool,
I'm heatin' up so make me cool.
So you sit on my knee and tell me that you love me,
But I know that you're joking cos I could never see,
That look in your eyes,
Oh you make me so high,
Just tell me that you want me and we'll be alright.

Hannah Clarke (13)

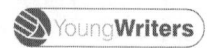

Dorothy The Great

Dotty makes pig noises
She's a staffie and she's rather happy
She's strong and courageous
But her fleas are quite contagious
We are potty about Dotty
But not when she eats the man off Monopoly
And eats him quite slobbery
She is a total hottie
That's our Dotty
Licking faces
Then licking her botty.

No, no, not Dotty
She's our number one spotty dog
And we love her forever
Because she is so blinking clever
And mad!

Olivia Faith Emmerson (12)& Arlo Emmerson-Hewitt (7)

History

Me and you are history
There's nothing more you could say or do
We died out, it's over
But I've gotta say goodbye
When we started we were fire
But it all had to stop
Now me and you are history
But the best never stops
We still live in memories
But this time it's gone too far
I love you with a new love from Haven
But it's all stopped now
Ooooh!

Chloe Mulholland (11)

Light At The End Of The Tunnel

When you wander on that long dusty road
With no one to hold
And no one to take your hand

When darkness shadows over you
And the rain pours over you
With no one to guide you through

Remember that rainbows shine out after every rainstorm
Remember that the sun shines out on every cloud day
Remember that fairy tales always have a happy ending
And there's always a light at the end of the tunnel . . .

When the silence suffocates you
And your world is black and blue
And everything has turned against you

Remember that rainbows shine out after every rainstorm
Remember that the sun shines out on every cloud day
Remember that fairy tales always have a happy ending
And there's always a light at the end of the tunnel . . .

Ahhh . . .

Remember that rainbows shine out after every rainstorm
Remember that the sun shines out on every cloud day
Remember that fairy tales always have a happy ending
And there's always a light at the end of the tunnel . . .

Ahhh . . .

Cathy Ross (16)

Hold On

I'm nothing less than terrified
That you might commit suicide
I know that if you were to die
I'd too - in no time - take my life
These thoughts keep rushing through my head
The visions of you lying dead
I'm guilty after every thought
And still I panic more and more
I have to get this off my chest
But that does not mean I can rest . . .

Please just be all right
I need to come home to your smile another night
Please just stay alive
I need to come home to your face another night.

How can I predict how you feel?
How can I tell when you're for real?
Please know I'll help you all I can
Offer more than a helping hand
I will always be here for you
I beg you to reply, 'You too!'
I know that you might get depressed
Unstable, insecure and stressed
But in these times you must hold on
Come on, I beg you because I know
I know you can be strong.

Rosalind Bruce (18)

Dear Nan

Laying in bed
Too weak to move
She gets worse and worse
I start to cry
Please Nan, don't die
Losing her hair
There is no cure
I'm scared and upset
She comforts me tightly
I have to go home
Let her sleep alone

I go back in the morning
The room is empty
Everyone is crying
My nan died.

Seven years gone past
I still miss her so
She haunts me forever
Never to go
I wish you were here
You missed all my life
I still love you Nan
I feel you holding me tight
It's time to say bye
I promise Nan I'll try not to cry.

Kirsten Mace (14)

Why?
(This song is dedicated to my hero, Michael Jackson, 1958-2009)

Why does everyone judge me? Why does nobody see?
That I am only human, I just want to be me
Why don't they see the music anymore, why do they criticise?
Why do the ones who once loved me, now have hatred in their eyes?
Why am I seen as the bad buy, when in truth, I am the victim?
My entire life's work is in jeopardy and the future's lookin' grim . . .
Why am I cooped up in a small dingy cell?
I'm not a criminal, why must I go through this Hell?
Why can't they see the truth? Are they blinded by the lies?
Can anyone really hear my lonely desperate cries?
Why must it be *me*, who has to face these allegations?
Why must it be *me*, who is humiliated in front of all the nations?
Is it because of my wealth, my power, my fame?
Is their sheer jealousy the *true* reason behind their claims?
Why is there no one there to comfort me, say that there's no need to cry?
Why do I feel so along now - *why, why, why?*
I feel like I'm dying inside, like I'm being ripped and torn apart
Why do they do this to me? Why do they break my heart?
They took my pride, they took my money
They took my soul and found it funny
They ruined my reputation and they ruined my name
They laughed in my face, as I got hurt and blamed
They killed me inside, but what hurt the most in the end
Is that I once thought that they were my friends . . .

Anneka Honeyball (14)

I Miss You

I miss you more than all my heart can say
I never wanted to leave you like this
I promised you I'd find a better way
The only way to leave was our last kiss

That memory of you I'll always store
A special place just for you in my heart
I'll never forget walking through that door
To leave you behind was only the start

You said that you would never forget me
But where will you be when I need you here?
With you is where I'll always want to be
Losing you now will always be my fear

You're something special, you're one of a kind
I miss you, you are always on my mind.

Holly Riordan (13)

Unsatisfied

I just don't understand
Everything that I wish for
Is nothing to do with who I am
'Cause if you're not my man
And I'm not going to do
Then I guess you need to know
That here's not the place for you
'Cause I need a man that doesn't
Leave me unsatisfied
Unsatisfied with love
A man who thinks I'm enough
Who comes to find me and when he does it's set me free
And he won't leave me unsatisfied.

Caitlin Kinney (13)

Bright-Coloured T-Shirts

I miss your smile
I haven't seen it in a while
Where did it go?
Did it fly way?
Is it lost in space?

What happened to your soul?
Why did you let it go?
Because now all it is
Is a black hole.

Your bright light has dimmed
Why won't you let me in?

Pull out your bright-coloured T-Shirts
And forget how much it hurts
Glow like a blue sky
After a rainy day
Live your life the way you wanna
And never ever let them bring you down.

Who are they to kill your dreams?
We've got ways and means
Of showing them who we are
They can love us or hate us
But they'll never break us
No, they'll never take us
Cos we were born to be who we are.

Lauren Wilkes (13)

Changing Heart

Stuck in my head again,
The visions will never change,
Your voice introduces the sweetest of nightmares,
Then something changed I was sure,
With your words burning in my heart and head,
Every time I try I know we will never part.

'Cause I know this is true,
I will never be able to leave you,
As if I had glued my heart to yours,
I know this is true I will never leave you.

I know that our strings will never untie,
As if the knot is a puzzle to undo,
Your face will stay in my life forever,
We've been together for too long to part.

'Cause I know this is true,
I will never be able to leave you,
As if I had glued my heart to yours,
I know this is true I will never leave you.

And when heaven calls we'll go together,
Be beautiful white angels forever,
Together till eternity.

I know this is true I will never leave you

Forever.

Zoë Powell (13)

My Amazing Little Light

I have a small eternal flame
And this little light of mine,
Even though it might just go . . .
It still is going to shine!
Freeing all of my worried thoughts
Inside my troubled mind
Burning on through rain and sun
Bringing peace to everyone . . .

Across the whole wide world it flows
Transforming people as it goes
Whizzes back in quite a race . . .
Making the world a better place!

The troops stop shooting
They make a truce
Poverty is cured
Trapped animals set loose
I'm so proud
I want to say it loud
And so does the goose and the poor old moose
Trapped and starved until . . .

Across the whole wide it flows
Transforming people as it goes
Whizzes back in quite a race
Making the world a better place!

Lily Potter (10)

Into The Light

I know that you're mad,
An wanna hit me iron clad,
I gave you excuses, I told you lies,
Your final shout was your final bye-bye,
It matters that you hear me,
So you're stayin' clear of me,
Cos I only opt one thing to say.

Chorus
You know I miss you,
An anything you say I'll do,
Just promise we'll keep together,
Through sunny or stormy weather.

Before we broke it was just you an me,
No cracks just harmony,
An every night I see the sight
Of you and me in the light,
But you're carrying half my heart,
An baby it's never been so dark,
So bring me to the light.

Chorus
You know I miss you,
An anything you say I'll do,
Just promise we'll keep together,
Through sunny or stormy weather.

Bethany Chipperfield (13)

Seraphim

Seraphim flying high, just beyond my reach
When I'm uneducated, you're the one to teach
When I'm feeling down, you're the one who lifts me high
But never close enough to be with you up in the sky.

Seraphim flying high
Always there and in my sight
Seraphim flying high
Through the day and through the night
Seraphim flying high
Dare not tell or speak your name
Seraphim flying high
For it would bring both our shame.

Seraphim flying high, laughing in a cloud
When I'm feeling meek you're the one who makes me loud
When I'm feeling sad, you paint a smile upon my face
But never long enough for me to run out of my pace.

Inside our ring of comfort
Our happiness spreads
If only I could muster the words
That would make a difference
Inside our minds, we create anything
Worlds are born at our command
And though we are companions
I am so alone.

James Williams (16)

Better Place

When the skies are dark and grey
Don't you want to brighten them?
Don't you want to make them blue once again?

When the flowers droop to the soil
Don't you want to give them a lift?
Don't you want to make their colours bright not dull?

I want to make the world a better place
I want to make the world a safer place
I want to make the world a nicer place
For you and for me

Say no to guns
Say no to knives
Say no to crime
Say no to things unsafe

I want to make the world a better place
I want to make the world a safer place
I want to make the world a nicer place
For you and for me

Say no, say no, say no to guns
Say no, say no, say no to knives
Say no, say no, say no to crime
Say no to an unsafe world
For me . . . and for you.

Samantha Smart (13)

Not Anymore

There was a story
That somebody told me
About this girl
Who met this guy
And when she saw him
She was flying high.

There was a song
That somebody sang for me
And when he sang
His voice was soaring free
Like you and me, used to be
But not anymore.

Oh why did this happen to us?
Just you and me, the perfect team

Do you remember the day I met you
In the hallway?
You smiled at me
It's the best memory.

You took my heart with just one kiss
Oh how could we see it ending like this?

Oh why did this happen to us?
Just you and me, the perfect team
But not anymore.

Megan Parkinson (13)

Different

Some people call me random
but I like it
I don't wanna fit in with the crowd
and I don't wanna change it one little bit

You know I really care about you
it's my life and I want it this way
there is nothing you can do
there is nothing you can say

Chorus
It's good to be different
I'm individual
I'm unique
I want you to remember me
every time I speak

I don't wanna be boring
and I want you to love me for me
I'm not like all the other girls
my love for you is free

You know I really care about you
it's my life and I want it this way
there is nothing you can do
there is nothing you can say

Chorus to fade.

Fleur Bowler (12)

Everything Changes But Beauty Remains

Something so tender I can't explain
My heart beating wildly like the wind in the sky
My heart never stops for you
So *boom boom,* get me out of this place
Now *boom boom,* it's burning like flames
Get me out on the count of three
One, two, one, two, three.
When we were young, young not too old
We shared a moment like this
Blossoms grow, roses too
That's like me and you.
So I say, everything changes but beauty remains
I know I cannot explain
But when you're gone I'll still remember you
That's like me and you
That's like me and you-u-u-u.

Francesca Stoddart (9)

Listen To My Heart

I looked up into the bright sky
And saw the stars as they glitter light
And I was wondering where you will be tonight?
I could scream out your name
But will you hear me?
It's breaking my heart
Tearing me apart
'Cause it's hard for you to understand.

Omolara Omoniyi (14)

Dance In The Rain

It might be a sudden clash of lightning
Or it could've been building for years
But it will relight your every worry
And all your strongest fears
You can run as fast and far as you like
But the storm will follow you
Turn and brave it, face its power
It's the strongest thing to do
Don't wait for the storm to pass
Learn to dance in the rain
There's nothing that can hold you back
Once you can manage the pain
Don't worry about doing it yourself
You'll never wake up alone and scared
I'll never leave you so long as you need me
You'll never have to feel like nobody cared
We can help you fight this
Trust me and take my hand
It's a tough journey through the rain
But when the storm gives up, you will understand
Don't wait for this storm to pass
We can learn to dance in the rain
Nothing will ever hold you back
Now that you have beaten your pain
Learn to dance in the rain.

Gabi Martin (15)

Wake Up!

In every area of the news, death, despair and fear
Linger round my head like a never-ending nightmare
Like a never-ending nightmare
Oh, oh, oh . . . c'mon now
Wake up, wake up
Have you even noticed
Or has it just faded into thin poisoned air?
Take some time and you'll see . . . why
Poisoned by the media, who do I believe?
Confusion reigns, heartbreak sure
And death numbers increase more and more
Oh, oh, oh, c'mon now . . .
Wake up, wake up
Have you even noticed
Or has it just faded into thin poisoned air?
Take some time and you'll see . . . why
Fightin' to protect
Are you betraying too?
Death collides with life
As our worlds are blown apart
Oh, oh, oh, c'mon now . . .
Wake up, wake up
Have you even noticed
Or has it just faded into thin poisoned air?
Take some time and you'll see . . . why . . .

Abigail Leighton (12)

Somethin' Great, Amazin' New

This ain't the way we like to live
Would like to give but cries and fibs
Control our lives like Labour, Libs
Have stole our pride and favour kids
With cash to burn, with no concern
For me, for you, for people who
Could maybe learn and maybe do
Somethin' great, amazin' new.

Crazy, true the way we work
Is through the dirt and days of hurt
When really all that we deserve
Is greener turf and peace on Earth,
I see the worth inside your eyes
So open wide your broken mind
And seek the times of peace and find
A place for you to cope with life.

Chris Driscoll (22)

Dreams Do Come True

Believe in yourself
Find your passion
Think positively
Play to win
Don't follow
Be number one
Don't lose sight of your goal
Give one hundred and ten percent
You have nothing to lose
You control your dreams
Dreams do come true
You've just got to believe in them.

Sara Siddiqui (15)

The Loner

I'm a loner
All because I'm a donor
I donated blood to save another
For her lover
Because her lover is my brother
I did it for my mother.

I was scared
But I never cared.

I made my mother proud
Then the bully got loud
Started hanging around
He was in with the wrong crowd
How could this be allowed?

I was scared
But I never cared.

Chloe Howard (14)

Poem Writer's Block

Poem writer's block, where your mind goes blank,
Your thoughts pack up and don't come back,
Thinking and thinking and thinking some more,
Thinking so hard your head feels so sore,
Taking a break to refresh your mind,
When you return your thoughts might be kind,
Downing some water to help power your brain,
Sometimes writing a poem can be a real pain,
But don't let it stop you from having a go,
If you do not try it, you will never know
So put pen to paper and soon you will see
You could write poems just as good as me!

Stephanie Kenna (12)

It's Over

Don't speak anymore
I'm sick of your voice
'Cause boy you're grown up
If you leave it your choice.

I won't hold you back
I won't beg you to stay
I'm not gonna fight
It's over anyway.

I know we were close
I'm not gonna lie
But we didn't end badly
We really did try.

When we failed to work
It caused us both pain
It's time to give up
Before my heart gets broken again.

Luisa Raucci (12)

The Sun

Oh the sun is out to play
Shines gracefully day by day
Oh thy love the sun
Oh thy love the sun
For it's ever out to play
For it's ever out to play.

Abbie Culf (12)

You Are The One And Only

I've been trying so long
I've been trying so hard
Just to figure it out
I don't know who to turn to
Don't know who to talk to
Don't know who to shout
'Cause I'll follow you
Till the end of the Earth and back around
You're the girl, why can't you see
That you are the only one for me?
I've been searching for too long to just find you
I've been waiting for you every day
Just to hear what you'll say
You are my one and only
When I see your face in that special place
Then you'll disappear from sight without a single trace
I know girl that you, like the way I do
I just hope that you can see
That I will love you forever and all eternity
You're the girl, why can't you see
That you are the only one for me?
Searching for too long to just find you
I've been waiting for you every day
Just to hear what you'll say
You are my one and only.

Ryan Lee (14)

Stereotypical

You're a chav
You're an emo
You're a geek
You're a weirdo
You're a snob
You're a freak
You're a tart, does that mean you even have a heart?
Does it mean you ain't smart?
You use words like quantum physics
And a regular know-it-all
Then why should you fall?
Why should you suffer day in and out?
So just shout
I'm not a chav
Or an emo
Or a geek
I'm not a weirdo
Or a snob
Or a freak
So what if I like rock music
So what if I can do mathematical equations
So what if I just wanna be good
I know I'm not always open quotes
'Cool' close quotes
I really don't care!

Alice Cracknell (16)

Believe

Everything is possible when you believe
It could happen anywhere to you or me
Believe in yourself right from the start
Have confidence, follow your dreams and never give up
Then one day you'll see you can be everything you ever wanted to be
Believe in yourself, believe in yourself
Don't let anyone ever put you down
Believe in yourself, believe in yourself
Let your faith lead the way and never give up
Believe in yourself cos I believe in you
Everything is possible when you believe
It could happen anywhere to you or me
Reach up to the sky and touch the stars
Then you will find everything you ever wanted
Is right in front of your eyes
Believe in yourself, believe in yourself
Don't let anyone ever put you down
Believe in yourself, believe in yourself
Let your faith lead the way
Then your dreams will come shining through
Believe in yourself, believe in yourself
Never give up cos I'll be there standing right next to you
Believe in yourself cos I believe in you
Yes, I believe in you, you, you
Oh I believe in you.

Kiya Burgess (13)

Before

Before you go
I want to say I'll miss you
Before you leave
I want to hug you one last time
Before you talk
I want to say I'll always listen
Before you're lonely
I'll come and visit you
Before you're sad
I'll cry with you
Because I'll always be upset when you're not near
Before you disappear
I want to say I love you
I need to say I love you
And when we meet again
Face to face
I'll hold you close
Never let you scare me again
I know you'll be safe
But it doesn't stop my heart
From aching
And every day I notice you're not around
I'll let the tears run down my face
I promise I won't stop them
Because they're my memories of you.

Chloe Runkee (13)

They'll Call If They Want To

Illness is closing down your lungs
Torturing, it becomes too much
Silencing the many words you've sung
Never again do they feel your touch

Time's up -
But you've already left this sinister world behind
All that's left is Victorian brickwork
Damaged and broken
Destroyed like your love

Three days left for you to suffer
They'll call if they want to
Three days left until you're gone
They'll call if they want to

Damaged and broken -
My Victorian brickwork fell apart.

Eleanor Spawton (14)

Far From Home

Far from home
I've been away too long
When I leave you behind
I know there's something wrong
But I can't stay
Must go away
Trapped in this nightmare
Yet another day
Trust in others
Only leads to deceit
And my heart
Can take no more of it.

Jarlath Hagan (16)

Now I Know

Now I know just who to believe
See now I see just what you mean
Waving goodbye as I watch you leave

Sex, drugs
Rock and roll
Speed, weed
Loses control

Me as a friend was there for you
Now you're gone, I'm left to cry
All those memories seemed to have died
Taking it back, one step at a time

Because now I know
Just what I see
Now I'm left standing
Wondering why, why, why?

Kayleigh Patchett (18)

Just Me

Seemingly lost in a class of my own
Seeking happiness I find myself reaching for my goals
I find myself now in a healthy balance
Between the old and new
And that's the way I intend to stay
A happy medium is reached
So that I can feel contended
I don't really care what others think
As I know I am unique
A special being
With a purpose
To be me and not another.

Jenna Rainey (16)

Have You Forgotten Your Truths?

People judge, they stare, desperately ready to pounce
Their vicious remarks ripping into my ears
Unloving and spiteful their words trickle and dissolve into my mind
Setting right into my eyes, later providing me with tears
They ridicule because they may be distressed or jealous
However, the words and abuse hurled at me still cuts like a knife
Slowly bringing me to my knees, raising questions and even more suspicion
My mind may be racing but I must remember the wisest of words
Be brave, be yourself, then let them judge
They may not see me as an equal person now, but soon they will
Who will come out on top?
I will proceed and win gracefully, dignity intact
I must never retaliate, I could never stoop so low
And to attack someone I didn't even know
Soon they will feel unbearable guilt and the heavy shame
Should I walk away even if they shout after me and keep my sanity?
Instead I can savour and satisfy my soul by asking calmly
'Darling
Dearest
Brothers
Sisters
You may be saddened, but do not bring me down
Let me help and we will discover your inner peace
But tell me now at this moment, look into your heart and ask,
Have you forgotten your truths?'

Sophie Grace White (13)

You Call Me A Lair

I'm tired of hanging around,
Waiting for something to happen,
So I slit my throat in the shower,
And drown in my own blood,
While thinking of all the ways,
This world makes me so afraid,
I see my life rushing by me,
All the secrets and lies revealing,
And In the mirror I can see my blue eyes fading into grey
And I can feel the darkness burn inside me
All the wasted hours waiting for love
It took me so long to realise
It's never gonna happen
And then a figure walks in
And my vision starts to fade
I heard a faint scream
And then I push it away
All I can see is black darkness
I think I'm asleep at last
Dancing with the Devil
And sleeping on black grass
I told you this would happen
I told you again and again
But you called me a lair
You would anyway.

Melanie Rumble (12)

The Music Of The Night

Make-up on, clothes at the ready
Jump in your car, music bumping
Pick up your friends, call Mr DJ
Model walk on, let's make an entrance
Dancing shoes, people's heads
Flickering lights, music on time
People jumping, people rocking
People making it
Now . . .
Jump to the music of the night
It will hypnotise you
Jump to the music
All your troubles will float away
Look at me, then you'll see
Me moving, me grooving
You'll see what's going on
The music of the night
The music of the night
The music of the night
The music of the night
Go to bed now, sweetie pie
Just remember the beat
If you think you're something special
Then look at me
Night!

Lauren McLaughlin (14)

A Loyal Promise

I'd swim across the ocean blue
All obstacles I would get through
I'd guide you through the darkest night
If you ever lost your sight
When you're down, stuck in a rut
Depend on me, I'll help you up
For you my hand is always here
To heal your pain and wipe your tears.

In me you can always confide
Whatever the dilemma, I'll stand by your side
When you're in trouble, I'll bail you out
Have trust in me, never doubt
When you're weak, when you're not strong
I'll always be here, I'll never be gone
Expect me loyal to the end
I'll never be your enemy, always your friend.

We're like blood-brothers, you and I
We are unbreakable just like Bonnie and Clyde.
I'll journey through all of your hurt,
You know I'll die keeping my word.
We made a promise, a pact, a seal,
We shook hands, we made a deal
And to that I must stay true,
When you need me, I'm here for you.

Ceri Davis

Pandora's Box

My butterfly wings won't take me very far
When I'm floating up there amongst the stars
Like Icarus and Daedalus they'll burn away
And I'll be left all alone again
Falling from the skies on a slippery slope
Catch me on a hook, on the end of a rope
A rope that's so strong, it'll pull me along
When everything else is lost and gone
Thanks to Pandora and her magic box
Filled with tricks and evil things
For giving us one thing that will light up the night
And make everything feel all right, hope
The sweetest thought is that every bad thing
Has a silver lining, like the clouds in the sky
Thanks to Pandora and her magic box
For showing us what we could have lost, hope.

Emma Henderson (15)

Rap Star

This is the rap star speaking
Hey listen out, hear me out
Carefully and I won't shout
I put together pieces of scrap
To make this rap
So listen
I like to mess around all the time
Making poems that always rhyme
If you like the poem then put it in the book
If not then just take a look
I'm not finished yet so stay where you are
And don't forget this is the rap star, rap star, rap star.

Kainaat Mahmood (12)

Teenage Life

People always talking down to you
Not sure which path to choose
Life's just one big crazy maze
Can't wait to move on from this phase.
Just wanna do the right thing
But feel like no one's listening
To what you've got to say
'Cause it's your life at the end of the day
Things never used to be this hard
Now you're not sure who you are
Do you turn right or left?
Not sure which is best
Just wanna do the right thing
But feel like no one's listening
To what you've got to say
'Cause it's your life at the end of the day.

Theresa Locock (15)

Never Again

You say things to me that I cannot accept
The amount of heartbreaks I have wept
This time you have gone at least too far
Across my heart you left a scar
Never again . . . will you try to speak to me
Never again . . . could you act like the man
You had always wanted to be
I trusted you
I loved you
But not anymore
You are not the type to be ever adored.

Sophie Forbes (13)

Wind And Rain

You walk into the room, it's full of air
You see everything flowing like my hair
Flowing circles so beautiful . . .
You're already in the room
Why are you here?
I've been waiting for months, even a year
I cannot confess my loneliness . . .
I know the difference between wind and rain
Not all about it seems the same
No one knows when the wind will be blowing
Only I know, no one cares anyway
Come on, make my rainy day
No one knows where the rain will be falling . . .
From the sky, from the moon, the stars
I'll move closer to where you are
Because I know . . . the difference . . .
Between wind and rain.

Adelaine Ingram (11)

It's Raining

It's raining in the sky and I don't know why
So I sigh
Then suddenly it was sunny
And I was confused
I was happy once again in my lonely life
Ohhh, mmm
Why does it always happen to me?
It just has to be reality
Me and you could never be
Because it's raining in the sky
And I don't know why, so I sigh . . .

Hannah Russell (10)

I Need You

I woke up this mornin'
Sky is blue
Wake up tomorrow
You can see me thought
There's o one that I need
As much as you
Someone to be there
An' babe, it's you.

I walk down the streets
Lookin' for you
Lookin' high an' low
Looking for you
As days pass by
Looking for you
Why can't you just wait there
Because I need you.

I woke up this mornin'
Sky is blue
Woke up tomorrow
You can see me thought
There's no one that I need
As much as you
Someone to be there
An' babe it's you.

Kieran Jones (14)

Connection

How can we feel so close when we're so far,
I can I feel your face even when it's not there,
That look in your eyes, they have made up my mind,
I know you and me, we're just meant to be, baby,

Chorus

*We got a connection,
I know through and through,
That me and you, our love is too good to be true.*

I sit all alone wondering what you're thinking,
My mind is saying no but my heart's saying go,
I am gonna follow my heart,
Cos I can't bare us apart,
Cos . . .

Chorus

*We got a connection,
I know through and through,
That me and you, our love is too good to be true.*

Now I know what to do,
There's no point sitting around and waiting for you,
I have to tell you how I feel,
Cos I know my love will be true,
Because we have a connection.

Chloé Branagan-Liddy (12)

Come Closer

Here I am
I come to you
Draw yourself close to me
I need you, I want you
You are my everything
Visit me tonight as my soul cries out
Come closer to me
Hold me tight
Never let me go
Never let me fall
When I think no one cares
I know that you care
When I feel down, you cheer me up
When I sense trouble, you give me peace
How can I possibly not want you more?
Come closer to me
Hold me tight
Never let me go
Never let me fall

Your light is what I need and
Your truth is what I seek
Never let me go
Never let me fall
Come closer now.

Nana Adwoa Asiedu (18)

Invisible

When I first saw you, thought I had a chance
Me and you at the next school dance
Voices become blurred, when I think of you
I'd be the girl who got the guy
Living my favourite dream, but that's all it is
Cos you're one of those guys
All I think about is you and your perfect smile
Yet you don't know my name
Why do guys like you
Always make me feel . . . invisible?
I'd be the envy of the girls
The quiet girl who got the popular guy
Teased by all my friends, cos I got a little crush
I got a feeling money couldn't buy
But it's just a stupid trance
Cos you're one of those guys
All I think about is you and your perfect smile
Yet you don't even know my name
Why do guys like you
Always make me feel . . . invisible?

Yeah, you're the one I dream about
Plan my life around
Yet all the guys like you
Always make me feel invisible, oh invisible.

Chloe Harris (14)

Perfect

Sometimes the rain just falls
Sometimes things just aren't meant to be
Sometimes I feel upside down
And so unhappy
But you turned my world around
The first time you looked at me
From now on the sun just shines
And everything feels so right
I never want to lose you . . .

You turned my world around
You make me smile when I'm down
Don't know what it is about you
But you're perfect, yeah.

Whenever we have a fight
You're the first to make things right
Any time I feel upset, then you come and hold me tight
I don't know what it is about you
You're just amazing
My everything.

You turned my world around
You make me smile when I'm down
Don't know what it is about you
But you're perfect.

Katrina Keatley (13)

I Wanna Be Grown Up

I wake up at quarter past six in the mornin'
Mum shouting at me, so borin'
I wish I could stay in bed
With the covers over my head
No one to tell me what to do or to say
'Cause I'm gonna go my own way.

I wanna be grown up
Do clubbin' instead of homework
Why walk when you can run?
Why not chase and have fun
All the time?

I'm awake but I'm sleepy
Most of my clothes don't fit me
Which is bad for a teenager
All my thoughts they fastly occur
I'm holding on but I wanna move on
Till I see the lights shine
I'm gonna party all night.

I wanna be grown up
Do clubbin' instead of homework
Why walk when you can run?
Why not chase and have fun
All the time?

Emily Ashmore (10)

Eternal

Happiness and sadness
summed up in the dying flight of a bird
Or a reflection on youth,
what has been and now is gone,
a lost summer's day,
a life spent looking back.
The destruction of our hopes
and the building of our dreams.
A memory held in our hearts forever.
Happiness and sadness summed up together,
they stand side by side, hand in hand forever.
Destroying our hopes is an easy thing
but building our dreams is harder,
but more worthwhile,
because you're the one that makes it happen.

(Piano solo)

A memory held in our hearts forever.

Martha King (12)

I Guess It's Over

We're here always together, but time and time I see you now
we're not together.
Days and days I just miss you and your funny smile, the way you talk, but . . . I
guess it's over.
I've seen you with your new girl. I don't care, I'll have to find a better someone.
So I guess me and you are over.
mmm . . . mmm . . . mmm . . . over
mmm . . . mmm . . . mmm . . . over.
I guess it's over.

Elle Reynolds (9)

For You The Sun Shines

When I see you I feel a pump in my heart
Know baby when I kiss you
My heart starts speeding like a rocket
It's for you that the sun does shine
Because of you I see the light
At the end of the tunnel
Yes, you're the one I treasure so much
I love you
Without question I love you
When I see you I feel a pump in my heart
Know baby when I kiss you
My heart starts speeding up like a rocket
It's for you the sun does shine
Because of you I see the light
At the end of the tunnel
Yes you're, the one I treasure so much
I love you
Oh yeah, I love you.

Nathan Adam Walters (12)

Perfect 10

From the crumpled up paper
To the ink from the pen
To the heart where it came from
To the tears that it sends
To the eyes that will read it
To the words that are meant
To that one single love
You're my perfect 10.

Adam Freeman (18)

Someday

I walked down that sweet road,
Dust filled the air as my feet touched the ground.
And everywhere I go,
The mem'ries of you, no they don't make a sound.
But I don't mind,
Let them all talk, I don't hear what they say,
Cos we will meet again, someday,
Someday . . .

I've got to go home.
Back to the place I have always belonged.
I've got to go home,
Back to the place I have always belonged.

I lie in the long grass,
The sun on my face and the wind in my hair.
And I, I sit and wonder,
What would life be like if you were still there.
Now everyone's staring as I walk away.
But we will meet again, someday.
Someday . . .

I've got to go home.
Back to the place I have always belonged.
I've got to go home,
Back to the place I have always belonged.

Zoe Peterkin (15)

Forbidden Love

If you're in love
And they love you
It could be right
Could not be true
It's forbidden love
A forbidden love
It's a forbidden love

My friends can ell
That something's up
But I can't say
That I'm in love.

Nobody would approve
Of my secret love
That's hidden away
From the world

Chorus

It's a star in the night
It's the rush of excitement
it's a thrilling ride . . .

Of a forbidden love
I have a forbidden love
So what about you?

Chloe Burrell (12)

The City Is Broken

The city is broken
Everyone is caught in a web of lies
They're full of deceit and torment
Now their souls are dropping like flies.

Just 'cause the power overtook you
Now your demons are plaguing the nights
Fair maidens bow down beside you
And they bathe in the milk of wolves.

For vampires they truly are
You now follow the path of the damned
Now you have lost your crown
And your heart beat starts to stop.

This is because you sold your soul
To the king of down below
For riches and gold
Your skin is now hard and cold.

So can you see what you've done
You've gone and made such a fool of yourself
Can you hear the cries of your past?

This is because . . .
The city is broken.
Broken.

Darcie Lowrie (12)

Without You

Yesterday, you told me that you loved me
So why have we grown apart?
How can I ever kick this feeling without you?
To hold me in your arms.

And I don't want to live my life without you
It seems like I'm just gonna have to.

When I think of the smell of your skin
Or the way I felt around you
But most of all the warmth of your touch
All these little things made me love you oh so much.

Now I don't know where I can go from here
When I think of you it brings me to tears
I thought your love for me was real
This is gonna take a time to heal.

Not much left to say but I'm doing this my own way
Forgetting all my memories with you
This is the only way I can cope
Cos I can't forgive you

Tomorrow I'll pretend you never loved me
And your face will be erased from my mind
But I can't ever kick this feeling without you
To hold me in your arms.

Jade Haley (14)

It's Raining Flowers In My Heart

It's raining flowers in my heart
Fragrance has taken over me and my life
Entering my heart and becoming my breath
You're the dream blooming in my eyes
You're a moon growing on me and taking over me
If water evaporates to become clouds,
Are you that blue fire?
Am I turning sweet and falling into the fire of love?
If water evaporates to become clouds,
Are you that blue fire?
Am I turning sweet and falling into the fire of love?
It's raining flowers in my heart
Fragrance has taken over me and my life
Entering my heart and becoming my breath
You're the dream blooming in my eyes
You're a moon growing on me and taking over me
You're a beauty with one eye oozing out nectar and another one wine
If the lips are nectar where is the honey?
Here are the flowers itself honey
It's raining flowers in my heart
Fragrance has taken over my life
Entering my heart and becoming my breath
If water evaporates to become clouds
Are you that blue fire?

Kisshanath Alankaratheepan (13)

The Lie

When we first met
It was love at first sight
In my long dark tunnel
You were the light
I was head-over-heels
I saw nothing wrong
If you were a singer
Then I was your song
But then I met her
Your beautiful ex
She told me about you
She said I was next.
'Get out,' she said,
'Before it's too late.'
I didn't want to believe her
And I was trapped so tight . . .
You're living a lie
I know you were lying
My heart was so strong
But now it is dying
We fell in love
Seemingly naturally
It took some time
But now I am free.

Samantha Bull (14)

Amnesia

I fell and hit my head
And now my brain is dead
I can't remember owt, what you on about?
Do I know you? What've we been through?
Who the hell am I?
I don't wanna hear these lies
I crashed my motorbike
Now I'm on a practise trike
I don't need a third wheel
Cos I'm the real deal
When I ride down town
I bring the world right down
I shouldn't be here
I wanna disappear

Nothing makes sense to me
I just need some company
Nothing makes sense to me
Amnesia's taking over me.

Ollivia Dale (13)

Untitled

Here we are once again
We're torn into pieces
Next time we meet
I'm sure you will feel the same as me,
The same small spark of happiness
That roamed my empty heart
And then you filled it with a huge giant snog!

Conner Doidge (14)

Burn The Skies

Sick living in a Third World town
Just to get away from it
Away from it

There is a fire, a fire beneath these feet of mine
And I'm gonna burn, burn, burn your ignorant skies
I wanna be blinded by those bright lights
I'm gonna start a fire and burn, burn, burn this town

No sir, I do not know why the caged bird sings
So can someone please explain to me?
Were your eyes sewn shut or do you believe?

There's something better than this, better than this, better than this
There's something better than this, better than this, better than this

There's gotta be something better than this
Better than this, better than you
I wanna be blinded by those bright lights
I'm gonna start a fire and burn, burn, burn this town
Just watch your ignorant skies burn orange and brown.

Laura Samuel (16)

I Thought The War Would End

I thought the war would end
But no that cannot be
For the war will never end
While guns and knives hunt me
I thought the war would end
But no that cannot be
For if I step outside this door
A bomb would fall on me
I thought the war would end
But no that cannot be
For only once the war has ended
Shall my mum come back to me.

Phoebe Corser (15)

Coma

Every time I think I'll die
I see a butterfly flutter by
With black steel wings and seething eyes
Why would an angel take this disguise?
And so I live to see another day
But who would have it any other way?
Not you perhaps, but I've waited too long
I wilt like a flower while others grow strong
The butterfly lingers and stalks my dreams
He wants me to eternally suffer it seems
And so I live to see another day
What can I give them to take me away?
I've lain in this bed for thirteen years
I cannot speak or move, but I still have my ears
I hear them whisper, 'Will he ever awaken?'
But their enduring hope I'm afraid is mistaken
And so I live to see another day
Why do they let me lie and decay?
Today the butterfly speaks to me,
'There is one way to set yourself free
You must open your eyes and look to the sky
There is no other way you can die.'
I obeyed the angel and embraced the light
I think I'll leave tonight.

Brendan Johnson (17)

Edgehill Battle

Riding through the dim-lit field,
as Prince Rupert my sword I wield.
Happy faces do I see,
among my men I lead to thee.
For I know and only I,
shall see the faces there to die.
Among the battlefield they'll fight,
to save our king today through night.
In my heart I feel the fear
no soldier I see shows it's here.
In my ear screaming men,
charging forth into the glen.
My horse a-galloping straight ahead,
my horse in front of the army in red.
My heart a-pounding with the beat
I charged away into the heat.
We soon retired back from the chase
our hearts were pounding from the race.
As silence fell upon the field,
the flags were lowered as my sword I wield.
Riding through the field to thee,
I see the faces I led to thee.
For I knew and only I
should see these faces there to die.

Beatrice Grist-Perkins (14)

Today

Yh in my hood all I see is little youths rollin' with knives,
see the elders getting locked up for gun crimes,
yh and that's why we need to get these weapons out the hood,
start it all over back to the way it should,
stop, say no to all the shanks and the glocks,
stop, say no to all the youths shooting green from their socks,
yh for all it's worth I ain't preaching,
I just write my rhymes and hope it's youths that I'm teaching,
'cause every day you hear on the news another youth dead,
yh why can't we change just like 2Pac said,
yh all I hear is *bang* another body's dropped,
another youth's life's been stopped,
yh all I see is shank being put in someone's chest,
left on the street pathway to rest,
yh for all you kids who think this is fun,
just think about the mother of the little daughter or son,
it just ain't fair to put people through this pain,
yh it just ain't fair I'll say it again.

James Hill (14)

Untitled

Don't forget to breathe slow
Close your eyes, take it slow
Count to 100 and smile
The sun is always shining
For another day.

Katie Thorne (15)

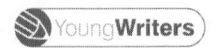

One Chance Only

A strange emotion you can't contain
You fight it, hate it and complain
But what use is that with a life like yours?
I'm telling you, the one you adore
But each day you scream, you cry and you curse
So why won't you write a draft of a verse
Or maybe a chorus you can sing with praise
And put an end to this petty phase?
You can do it, I love you, I know
Or else this pain you feel won't go
So go out and sing it, make others cry
Or you'll be hurting until you die
'But how can this finish?' I hear you say
'This will always end in dismay
The truth will be told, the word will be out
That all I can do is cry and shout.'
But this, my dear, is a transient phase
For us both soon to enter a new age
Of an entirety of sheer bliss
Without the tears or hunger or fists
But until then life must avail
Or else our purpose, here will fail
So release hurt and hatred from your mind's eye
And make a little music every day till you die.

Emma Craddock (17)

Sing Into My Microphone

It started off with just me and you
Now we're together I don't know what to do
You never call me up on the phone
I always tell you that I feel alone
So sing into my microphone
Say anything you want
Say that I need you, say that I love you
Cos now I feel the same
I really love you but we just can't go on
It doesn't feel like this is my home
You never tell me you love me now
You used to say it, I felt so proud
So sing into my microphone
Say anything you want
Say that I need you, say that I love you
Cos now I feel the same
You make me feel so insecure
When you said you loved me, were you sure?
I always told you I loved you more
Than anything I've ever seen before
So sing into my microphone
Say anything you want
Say that I need you, say that I love you
Cos now I feel the same.

Kirstie Hember (13)

Wind Song

When the wind blows
The quiet things speak
Some whistle
Some sing
Some shriek
Doors bang loud
Flowers swish
Leaves blow
Children make a wish
Fires spark
And spit out ash
Foxes howl
Wind must dash
Now the wind stops
Suddenly
Then
The quiet things
Are silent once again.

Georgia Kirk (11)

Take It And Break It

Why don't you take it and break it
Because it's never gonna be the same?
I've waited all my life, but to my surprise
You're never gonna change again
You're never gonna change again.

Kerrie Arnold (12)

One In A Million

Lying on my bed, thoughts running through my head
of when it was me and you
I got this feeling running through my veins
and it's making me lose control.

Chorus

Cos you don't know what you're doing to me
Cos baby you, you're one in a million
you're the one that I want, the one that I need
and I don't wanna let you go.

It's so hard to think, so hard to feel without you by my side,
If this is how it feels, then this is how I wanna feel
about you every single day of my life.

Chorus

Cos you don't know what you're doing to me
Cos baby you, you're one in a million
you're the one that I want, the one that I need
and I don't wanna let you go.

Repeat chorus.

Cos you're the one that I want, the one that I need,
cos baby you are . . .one in a million
and I ain't never letting you go!

Charlie Schofield (14)

Chris Brown Your Man Ain't Me - Reply
'So What, My Man Ain't You'

Boy I bet that you think
You really know my man
But he ain't like you
And I know that he really loves me
He may sometimes be rude
Give me some attitude
But I know deep down how he really feels
But I bet you been thinkin'
That I'm gonna dump him for you
But it ain't gonna happen boo
Get it in your head
You wanna take me away
Well listen up, cause I gotta say
is it gonna happen? Answer, no way
Stop creepin'
I got a man that yes, I'm keepin'
And you ain't gonna get in the way
Boy, I got my man, can't you understand that I love him
And he loves me, forget what you see
Stop trying to tell me that it's bad the way he's treatin' me
He gets angry and yes, I'll admit that is true
But boy, please, so what, my man ain't you.

Sherri Lewis (17)

We're Gonna Get Ya

A long time ago
You called us names
Picked on us and made our life Hell
Now the tables have turned my friend and

We're gonna get ya
We're gonna get ya good
We're gonna get ya
And get our revenge

You may think we're bluffing
That we're pulling your leg
But, let me tell you
We're not, we don't joke and

We're gonna get ya
We're gonna get ya good
We're gonna get ya
And make you regret everything you said.

And as you start to flee
Leaving dust in your wake
We'll be right behind you
You can't run forever
And when you finally stop
We're gonna get ya!

Corrinna Osborne (14)

Be Someone

Hey Bub, get out of the club and in the car
He's pulling a knife, which he just took your wife's life with
You can see it's just been done
What are you gonna do because you can't run?

When it started in the beginnin'
I'd never have thought I'd be winnin'
But look at me now, you'll go wow
When it started in the beginnin'
I'd never have thought I'd be winnin'
But look at all my women.

Why is it so hard to be someone when you wanna be someone
With all the threats you get and all the bad vibes you get?
Why is it so hard to be someone when you wanna be someone?

When I get this crap I just think
Why is it so hard to be someone when you wanna be someone?

When it started in the beginnin'
I'd never have thought I'd be winnin'
But look at me now, you'll go wow
When it started in the beginnin'
I'd never have thought I'd be winnin'
But look at all my women
So now I'm guessing it's time to get off this ride.

Oliver Redmond (12)

Stay With Me

Ooh baby you're my cherry pie
I love it when you look at me
like I'm the apple of your eye
You make me feel so happy inside
when all I really want is you to be with me

Chorus

Oh baby, just stay with me
Stay with me
Baby never leave me
Just stay with me

Ooh baby I love you with all my heart
and when I saw you with that girl
it was like an arrow through ma heart
baby never let me see that again

Chorus

So stay with me baby
never let me go
'cause I wanna let you know
I'm never gonna let you go
and all I wanna say is

Chorus.

Sarah Campbell (14)

We Both Know!

Lost for words
I scribble down the line in my heart
I know it hurts
Reminded of the time when we're apart
I would scream out your name
But I'm too scared someone will hear me
By mistake.

And you're inches away and my heart starts to shake
Your hand close to mine, almost touching
You look in my eyes and you know that it's time
And we both know this is right.

I still claim
You should have been taken by surprise
And it's a shame
Because I know that she's the one to call you mine
And I'd say your name
But promise me you won't make me say it again.

And you're inches away and my heart starts to shake
Your hand close to mine, almost touching
You look in my eyes and you know that it's time
And we both know this is right
So right.

Nina Prells (15)

Fire Brigade

My tears are burning down my cheek
Burning, stinging as they have all week
Those things you said were not too kind
But neither are you.

Those tears are burning holes in me
Setting fire to everything you see
Please now pick up the phone
And call the fire brigade.

I need them to set this fire out
Fire out
Please.

I need them to set this fire out
Fire out
Please.

My tears are burning down my cheek
Burning, stinging as they have all week
I think now they'll go on forever
Unless you call the fire brigade for me.

Francesca Vinall (12)

Pretty In Pink

I like looking pretty in pink
But oh, I wish I was just a little punk
Cos I am more than mad about music
But oh, I'd like to *dance and sing*
Looking pretty in pink, pretty in pink.

Kerry-Ann Collar (9)

The Game

Your words used to drive me completely insane
Every day I fought the same old pain.
The burning hole in the centre of my broken heart
I hoped that a new day would never start.
I'd cut myself to put the pain on the outside for a while
And try to end my life prematurely, a thirteen-year-old child,
No matter how hard I tried to prove myself to you
The message just didn't seem to be getting through
I wasn't perfect, no, not even close
I wouldn't have been the daughter you would have chose,
If you had a choice, but you did not
Unhappy as it makes you, me, that's who you got,
So I came to terms with the fact that I wasn't good enough
I built myself up and made myself tough
I found a bridge and got over my fear
And after that day I never shed one more tear
I realised that I was much better that what they had said
And started to live for myself instead
Now I'm at the point
Where I'm all I can be
So be horrible and throw what you want at me
A fist, a bottle, another disgusting name.
Cause I've grown strong enough to play the game.

Lynsey Ann Petrie (14)

Unanswered Questions

How could you do this to me?
Leaving me here on my own
With nothing to do, just writing this song
About what you've done, leaving everything behind
But I don't know what you've got to hide.

Why did you go and never come back?
Is it because you couldn't face the facts?

I'm lying here awake, in the middle of a storm,
Hoping you'll be back, knocking on my door
But life's too complicated, that's for sure
So I doubt I'll be seeing you anymore.

Why did you go and never come back?
Is it because you couldn't face the facts?

You've left me here, in this empty room,
If you wait long enough, it'll be my tomb.
Since you've gone, everything's turned to grey
So now, I think, *I'm going to walk away*

And never come back, never come back
Only because I can't face the fact
That fact that you've left me, left me alone
Left me alone, writing this song.

Louise Smith (14)

These Teenage Years Of Mine

I look out the window
Look into the rain
Why does this teenage pain
Never go away?

I try not to argue
All I wanna do is
Make my point to you.

Are you listening to me?
Turn around and listen
Cos I wanna tell you
In these teenage years

I try not to argue
All I wanna do is
Make my point to you.

You make so many mistakes
Through these teenage years
You'll do all right when I'm gone
Without me beside your side.

I try not to argue
All I wanna do is
Make my point to you.

Chloe Fitzsimons (15)

Traveller's Tale

While I'm walking by the roadside
As the sun goes down
Marching on my two feet
To places seldom found.

When summer
Or winter comes again
I'll see you soon my friend, my friend.

People tell me that I'm a fool
And I won't get far
But I tell them I'm happy like this
Just me and my guitar.

When summer
Or autumn comes around
Places lost will be found, found.

Ancient forest all around me
Mystic link to the past
Chanting voices on the whispered wind
Telling tales of their craft.

When summer
Or winter comes again
I'll see you soon my friend, my friend.

Joe Hollamby (15)

My Jelly Belly Song

I'm not fat and I'm not thin
But how come I eat everything?
Once food goes down my hole
I think, *oh where's the other five bowls?*
I know I'm weird but I'm confused
If I was so hungry I'd even eat the news!
I went to the doctor and this is what she said,
'Now the thing is you just have to stay in bed.'
So I stayed in bed for a couple of hours
Then I thought I could watch Austin Powers
Halfway through the film my belly started to rumble
So I said to myself, 'Shall I have an apple crumble?'
Then my mum came in whilst I was stuffing my face
She said, *'Get up, get out, you're a disgrace!'*
I felt really bad so I didn't each brunch
I didn't even touch my banana bunch
From that day forward I was on a diet
And I'm surprised it didn't cause a riot
My mum and dad got used to it for a couple of weeks
Only because I was living off chicken soup and leeks!

Chanelle Andrews (13)

Mind Made Up

You want your privacy,
but that should never apply with me
you're close to me one minute but not the next
see, that's what happens when you're stuck in the middle.
Can't go left, can't go right
straight forward seems much easier
walking right out of your life
to someone else, to something else
something more than what's here
somewhere where there is no fear
to say what I think or feel
forever constricting what I say
so that I don't hurt your gentle ways
every day stepping on thin ice
I'm tired of always having to think twice.
So, finally when I fall
the tension can be taken no more
down into the blistering water
- relationship over -
many memories shattering into a million pieces.
No, just a person in the back of my mind.
A closed door, locked and sealed.
The contents of this room never to be revealed.

Buki Fatuga (16)

Falling In Love

I love the way you smile and laugh
You're made for me, we're the perfect match
When I'm with you I feel so attached
You complete me and that's a fact
Babe, I'd do anything for you
Without you my heart'd be in two
Yeah, we argue but we always pull through
That's why I'm always gonna be your boo
We stay up all night on the phone till late
When I go to meet you I just can't wait
I swear down this love was bought by fate
Would never be the same if we was mates
We go together like vodka and lemonade
I need you like a granny needs a zimmerframe
Me without your love would be so strange
I love you babes, so never change
Since I met you my heart's been fixed
Our love's so strong, it's like a ton of bricks
Guess we're just the perfect mix
We love each other with a passion
Don't feel real, feels like magic
Without each other it'd be tragic
Honest to God, I wouldn't be able to hack it.

Anya Holland (14)

What To Write?

Sitting here wishing I knew what to write
Somehow, in my brain, there's nothing in sight
Love's on all the song lists but somehow not on mine
I don't get it, usually it's meant to chime
But for me a song's a year-long something
I do in front of a mirror
Or I don't know what to say anyway
All I want is my songs to go far
I love to dance and sing
But today my lyrics don't ring
All I need is two more sentences and an ending
But right now my poem is descending
I need a song to make you cheer
I need a song that you can hear
But now I need an ending
I hope my poem's good depending
I spelt these words right
But I have decided not to write this poem all night
So now my song's done
But somehow I know I haven't won.

Emily Rose Derrick (10)

Past Twenty

I'm already fifteen but going on fifty-one
Then I wonder where my life has gone
Then I look back and say it's pretty grand
The only thing is I'm almost old
She has a child but she's seventeen
She had her whole life ahead
But now she's always busy
Then I remember
How common it is these days
You look in the mirror
And you almost cry
You wonder why you look like you're nineteen
You think about Botox
And all that plastic on your nose
So you can look only like you hit thirteen
It's probably fair to say
That when you're past twenty
They call you old
And they call you grey
You start to lose all your mind
When you realise you don't have much time
So say your goodbye
And just sigh.

Scott Milne (15)

My Heart

Just skips
A beat
Every time
I look at you
And I
Don't know why
But
I really want to
Know
No, no, no, no
Please don't tell me
Because baby if you tell me
Then maybe I'll wake up
From the dream
Do you
Think that
This could be real?
I just
Really
Want to
Know
How you
Feel.

Louisa Sham (16)

You Got Me Now!

Love me like a full-time lover
Love me like forever and ever
Show me what you're made of
And get your loving back
Show me what you're made of
And chuck that out
You don't need him as much as he needs you
Show him what you're made of and chuck him out
Your heart's been skipping the beat
Sure ain't because of him
Show me what you're made of and chuck him out
If you pass him on the street
Just walk on by
Because you showed him what you're made of
And chucked him out
You got me now
You don't need him because you got me now
Love me like forever and ever
You got me now
You got me now!

Kerry Spillane (16)

Untitled

Eleanor's a star
She's the best by far
Listen to the beat
It will make you move your feet
So get out on that dance floor
Come on what are you waiting for
I will have you begging for
More, more, more!

Eleanor Rose Bumby (8)

Messed Up

Messed up
The best way to describe it
Like a pool of water
Muddied by a child's footprints
Messed up
The best way to describe it
Like fresh bread dough
Ruined in the oven
Messed up
The best way to describe it
Like a beautiful summer's day
Threatened by a thunderstorm
Messed up
The best way to describe me.

Hannah Taylor (17)

Boxing Boots

Laces, Leather, tell me about your night
Heartache, broken, baby have you seen the fight
Me and you in shiny suits
Sugar, could you pass me my boxing boots

If I'm up against the ropes
You'll grab me by the throat
If I'm on the floor
You'll be begging for the second round

Lace, leather, tell me about your night
Heartache, broken, baby have you seen the fight
Me and you in shiny suits
Sugar, could you pass me my boxing boots.

Rhys Clarke (16)

Smokers

Smokers, smokers
They are always jokers
They're going down town
To hang around
Heart disease and cancer
Will grow on you
Smokers, smokers
They're going to choke us
Can't you see a cigarette
Is full of nicotine?
It causes you a lot of harm
And you lose your charm
Smokers, smokers
Cough, cough all over us
You'll never have any cash
To go to that bash
Fags in your pockets
Followed by soothing Lockets
Smokers, smokers
Jokers, jokers
Choke us, choke us
Cough all over us
Smokers, smokers.

George Bowman (12)

Love

What is the thing that gets two people together,
do you know what this is called,
have you experienced emotion?

Chorus

What is love?
Show me love,
let me know what love is,
since I have not experienced it.

Now I have a brief understanding of love,
but I do not have a complete definition
of the emotion love.

Chorus

Tell me does anyone know,
the complete definition of the emotion of love
because I need to know how it goes.

Love, it can make you happy,
or it can make you be upset,
you choose what you make
of the entire emotion called love.

Repeat chorus - Tell me x 3.

Emily Deborah Webb (16)

Times Are Changing

Times are changing, fast-rearranging, slow things down for me and you,
Don't live a lie in this weary world, stand on your feet and take the load,
Just where in the world are we going to?

When life's too tough and things get rough, carry on . . . just carry on . . .
The next day may be a complete mystery, but carry on . . . still carry on . . .

Times are changing, fast-rearranging; we'll just have to find a brighter day,
When love's not lost or fading away, wishing happiness for you and me,
A day to lead us where we want to be.

When life's too tough and things get rough, carry on . . . just carry on . . .
The next day may be a complete mystery, but carry on . . . still carry on . . .

Times are changing, fast-rearranging, look to the future come what may,
Don't dwell on mistakes of yesterday, tomorrow will lead us where we're going to be,
Bringing happiness for you and me.

When life's too tough and things get rough, carry on . . . just carry on . . .
The next day may be a complete mystery, but carry on . . . still carry on . . .

Times are changing, fast-rearranging; in view there is a brighter day,
Now the storm has gone away, love will always pull us through,
Never give up hope for me and you.

Now we know just where we're going to . . .

Tommy Birchall (15)

The Most Of Love

I opened my heart and let you in
Maybe a relationship could begin
But you spent each and every day
Asking will I be okay?
I replied with a smile but dying inside
Dying to say I couldn't love you
More than I do and it's the truth

I will miss those big brown eyes
Those tales and dramatic lies
For I will have to leave you never to return again.

So let's make the most of it
Let's make the most of it
Let's make the most of love
Before I have to go
Before my heart's had too much
Before I start to cry
Because I love you so much
Because leaving you don't get much harder that this
Because loving you gave me such bliss
So let's make the most of it
So let's make the most of it
So let's make the most of love.

Caitlin O'Riordan (15)

Time And Time Again

These cuts I have, all they need
Is love to help them heal,
Even the right romantic line
Can't prove the way I feel,
Come back baby, say you love me,
Don't stay away too long,
Tell me you'll be thinking of me
Each time you hear this song.
Time and time again
The chance for love has passed me by
And nobody can make me feel the way I feel,
Please don't let our flame die out
Since I saw you walk out my front door
I haven't stopped thinking for evermore.
Come back baby, say you love me
Don't stay away too long.
Tell me you'll be thinking of me
Each time your hear this song.
Time and time again
Please don't let our flame die out.

Thomas Bayliss (15)

Summer Nights

We walked along the riverbank
And sat upon its edge
We gazed into each other's eyes
Until the sun went blank
The night-time came, I lay alone
My dream was nearly gone
My heart sank low as the day woke up
A sadness in my heart
My love was gone
My heart was low
My life was not my own

You walked away, gone forever
I tried to move along
Thought I saw you in the distance
Only to be disappointed
It was another

Days passed by
Time moved on
But my heart was mending
I'd finally moved on
My love had changed
For the better!

Lauren McFarland (13)

Lonely Days And Empty Nights

It's 7pm
And you're not here again
Didn't think you would come
Leavin' me cold and numb.

So you're with her again
Oh my friends were so right
It's more sad lonely days
And more cold empty nights.

Oooh, I don't need you baby
Oooh, I won't wait for you to phone
Oooh, I don't want you baby
Oooh, don't bother to come home.

Took the bus to the station
Cos I need a vacation
I'll go where my heart takes me
Ain't gonna wait for you to break me
Again and again.

Oooh, I don't need you baby
Oooh, I won't wait for you to phone
Oooh, I don't want you baby
Oooh, don't bother to come home.

Ashleigh Pagani (17)

Lies - Life

If I cut myself, will I bleed the truth?
Will I find what I'm looking for on top of the roof?
I push out these thoughts only to see your face
Your eyes so full of deceit and grace
You're like the problem I don't want to go
Like the seed that I regret to sow
I can form my plans, I can wish you dead
But that still means that you're in my head.

I catch a glimpse of you, your subtle smile
An expression that paralyses from a mile
The damage is done, I have dug my hole
I look in your eyes, you know you have control
Wherever I go, it's the worse place to hide
Memories of you that I will never confide
'Cause I have no one, no friend, allies
Should I take my life and take to the skies?

A turn of the cloak
A glint of the knife
How long is it before
Lies become life?

Marley Fancourt (16)

Shooting Star

The sun's bursting in, I lie awake, can't wait for the new day to start
Feeling in my head I am clear, in my mind I'm alive
I'm in love, I can feel it in my heart
The day opens up on my world like a dream and I start to smile
This thing I have with you is not a feeling, a sense, it is more like a state of mind

Wherever you go I will follow, I just wanna be where you are
Like a shooting star, you shine brightest of them all
Wherever you go I will follow and it doesn't matter how far
Like a shooting star, you shine brightest of them all.

Once I was torn, I was lost
I didn't feel like me until I found you
This love is just like flashes of light streaming throughout my heart
Like a breath of fresh air, like a natural high
I lose sense of time
This thing I have with you is not a feeling, a sense, it is more like a state of mind.

Wherever you go I will follow, I just wanna be where you are
Like a shooting star, you shine brightest of them all
Wherever you go I will follow and it doesn't matter how far
Like a shooting star, you shine brightest of them all.

Hayley Garner (14)

Steel Blue Eyes

Looking up at the stars reflected steel blue,
Every time I close my eyes all I see is you.
Instinctive words with passion lost,
The lines I never spoke but heard,
All the years that time forgot,
I never knew the right word.

Because you were just like me
With your head in the clouds,
And your eyes full of mystery,
And we, we would live forever
Just you and me and the whole wide world to see.

And even now I hide
The tears for so many years I denied
If I could just find the right words
To tell you goodbye . . .

Because you were just like me
With your head in the clouds,
And your eyes full of mystery,
And we, we would live forever
Just you and me and the whole wide world to see,
Yeah you and me, and the whole wide world to see.

Freya Nicholls (14)

Trust Me

It's hanging in the city lights
Can you get it right?
And when I sing along
My life falls out of sight
Is that what you want
For me?

But, now the atmosphere
Is coming down to nothing more than empty air
As we hang in the moment
'Cause there's something there
Then we let it slide
Like the ghosts we pretend to be

Now, our hearts are coming undone
Like a crystal heartbeat
Washed up on a rock beach
I just can't get away
From the whispering names
The things that they say
But we don't have to listen another day
We'll find a way
Just trust me.

Rachel Finn (15)

Summer, Summer, Summer

Summer, summer, summer, that's right,
Summer, summer, summer, come on.
Wherever you may be, it's time for summer fun,
Sun, sea, sand, flow . . .
Let's go!
Holidays are what summer's all about,
Whether it's Spain, France or down the road,
It's time for
Summer, summer, summer, that's right,
Summer, summer, summer come on.
No need to worry now, the stress is all gone,
All that's happening is the fun going on.
No homework, no teachers, no bullies too,
As time goes by what you gonna do?
I know what I'll do - have some fun,
As long as this summer's going on,
Because . . .
Summer, summer, summer, that's right,
Summer, summer, summer, come on.
I don't know about you but I'll be having fun,
And as I do I'll be singing this sung!
3 . . . 2 . . . 1 . . . summer!

Shauna Burgess (13)

Revenge

Many broken windows
tennis balls landing on the floor
each one contains a message
not to be ignored
Battered chairs and tables
scribbles on the wall
guess you know my reasons
guess you got every call
I'm past reasoning with you
after all the things you said and did so
this is your flat, this is your flat
Well, that's what you get for talking to me like that
I'm past listening to you
and now we're done
and now we're done
I should have known before we began
that you would cheat, that you would lie
that you would make me cry
So I got my revenge
you will never hurt me again
you will never hurt me again
you will never hurt me again.

Aylish Gray (14)

My Share

Making space for the heartache
Letting go, don't wanna see your face
Again
Not looking back along my tracks
No need to know I'm not cutting any slack
Again
What you did to me changed everything
Even if you're hearing this, I know you don't care
Just look at what you've done
But we've finished it now
Moving on to a new place
Forgetting you, I don't see what's wrong with that
Get a home and call it my place
Paint it black, I erase the memories with that
Yeah
What you did to me, changed everything
Even if you're hearing this, I know you don't care
Just look at what you've done
But I've finished it now, don't care if you have
I'm alone, in a new world, facing straight
But I know I've had my share of you
And that's enough.

Hannah Fox (11)

Veggie Volume

The strum of a guitar, the flap of a bird,
The ticking of a clock and a dribble of gravy,
How many meals can I go through
Without you eating the beef?
How many nights can I spend eating pork chops on my own . . . ?
You're a veggie! And I don't know what to do,
You're a veggie, oh no, no meat for you,
Grab me a burger full of meat, and I'll try to tempt you baby,
Oh I love meat, and you need to love it too,
But . . . you're a veggie! And I don't know what to do,
You're a veggie! Oh no, no meat for you,
How about lamb? How about pork?
What about duck or a big fat turkey?
But no - because . . . you're a veggie! And I don't know what to do,
You're a veggie! But I'm coming after you.
I'll force feed you a slab o' cow, and maybe you'll be like, 'Wow!'
I love meeeat! Give me some more and get rid of the carrots!
But he'll still eat cabbage, because it's fab,
And he'll maybe have a couple of sprouts,
Because . . .
He's a rabbit! Oh yes . . .
He's a rabbit!

Amanda Hall (16)

Untitled

Faith, faith
You keep us safe
oh God
I love you
I pray for those who cannot see
Pull the veil from their hearts
Help them to see and believe in You God
When you read this you will see
God has been helping me
Through times of difficulty
My Bible is my sword
Forever I will love the Lord
He will guide me through my life
Even through my toughest strife
Jesus died and saved us all
He will catch me if I fall
I can always trust in Him
His love for us will never dim
If you want to lose your sin
You have got to trust in Him
So don't forget what I say
All you have to do is pray.

Lucy Paisley (13)

The End

Time, endless time
you wasted all those years of my life
and how I felt like giving up,
I now see, how things add up.

I tried to listen,
but all I could see was you and her.
I tried to focus
but all the lies were just too much.

What about me?
Think about what you have done.
What about us?
The memories will live on.

And I have never felt more alone,
on you, I thought, I could always depend.
I guess the time is up
but I never want the story to end.

What about me?
Think about what you have done.
Think about us,
the memories will live on!

Sarah Russell (13)

Things Will Turn Out Right

One night I was walking around
About to give up on everything
And I looked up at the stars
Then you looked down at me and began to sing;

'Well now, life at the moment
It may all be very rough
But you gotta keep on going
You can still remain tough.

You've got to keep on trying
You've got to put up a fight
But all I know is someday
Everyday will be all right.

I may not be here with you
I'm your angel in a star
And when you smile at me
I can see you from afar.

So you must never give up trying
Things will turn out right for you too
All I need you to remember is
I'll be right here beside you!'

Hayley Stronge (11)

Start Anew

I'm soaring with the highest mountain
I'm gliding with the highest cloud
I'm dancing on the moonlit pavement
I'm singing my song out loud.

I don't care who hears it
You need to know my point of view
This is our world, don't destroy it
Let's stop and start anew.

Imagine if there were no mountains
Soaring way up high
Imagine the highest cloud
Not gliding in the sky.

We're soaring with the highest mountains
We're gliding with the highest cloud
We're dancing on the moonlit pavement
And singing this song out loud.

We don't care who hears it
This is our point of view
This is our world, don't destroy it
Let's stop and start anew.

Amber Simpson (13)

All I Wanna Do

I take a breath of the air,
Open the door and step outside.
I see you walking down the street,
Then my heart skips a beat . . .
But I'm alright.

Chorus
All I wanna do is say thank you,
For all the things you did for me.
All I wanna do is see you . . . again,
But now it's my turn . . .

I'm sorry I didn't listen,
I'm sorry I shot the gun.
Just believe I didn't mean to hurt you . . .
Oh ohh.

Chorus
All I wanna do is say thank you,
For all the things you did for me.
All I wanna do is see you . . . again,
But now it's my turn . . .

I'm sorry.

Abigail Irvin (13) & Marc Irvin (12)

My Senses Are Fading, This Is All I Feel

If you told me you could kill this longing,
I don't know what I'd say,
It tears and rips my insides about,
It never waits for the dawn of the day,

But what if it's all that I know and all I can feel?
I never want to feel nothing again,
The first time around almost murdered me,
I'd be dead if it weren't for this pen,

Don't say the magic words, I'll push you away,
For fear of not longing any more,
But when I saw your face and looked in your eyes,
Was it that same longing that I saw?

What if I'm reading this feeling wrongly?
Maybe it's not meant for you,
What if it's just the hunger screaming?
Feed it I will not do,

I'm not ready for the longing to die,
Leaving only emptiness inside,
For now I will try to disappear,
For now I will just hide.

Cherish Thorpe (14)

Save Me

You need to talk before you explode,
Bottled up feelings cause mental overload
You want to say that you're running away.
Maybe tomorrow, maybe today.

Deep inside, your heart is bleeding,
Eyes are weeping.
You want someone to set you free,
To let you go, to leave you be.

You want to cry your feelings out,
There is so much to feel bad about.
But who will listen to worthless you?
When you're lost and don't know what to do.

Too many times you have been hurt,
And taken so much of this dirt.
No one seems to understand,
You need someone to hold your hand.

You want somebody to see you through,
Just one question, that is; who?
If someone would just hold you tight,
And let you know it will be alright.

Laura Smart (17)

I Wish

I'm thinking of you all the time
And I'm missing you every day
This world seems wrong without you
We treated you bad, there's a price to pay.

I wish I could tell you how much I need you
I wish I could say how much you mean
I wish you could know it's tearing me apart
Leaving me with nothing but an empty heart.

Hearing your voice inside my head
As if from a distant fantasy
Awaking to the cruel reality
That we'll never hear that voice again.

With all that passion and that strength
You tried to heal the world we're in
Now I wonder if you know
You really made a difference.

There's no way of knowing what went on
What thoughts were running through your head
But we took you for granted
And we lost the best thing that we had.

Paige Harper (17)

On My Shoulders!

If I was in danger, would you save me?
If I called your name, would you ignore me?
If I met a dragon would you pull out your sword?
If I was cold, would you put your jacket on my shoulders?
If I stand on top of the world
The highest mountain
Take the wrong turn
Will you come rescue me
And put your jacket on my shoulders?

If Aladdin took me off on his carpet
Would you do all you could to get me back in your arms?
Would you keep me safe?
Keep me warm by putting your jacket on my shoulders?
Then one day you picked me up
I deliberately wore a skinny, skinny top
Then it started to rain
You wore two jackets and said my name
I answered you of course
You took one of your jackets off with force
'You're special, not like girls I've met.'
Whilst you said this I felt your jacket on my shoulders.

Anna Helen Heywood (12)

Prose Or Poetry?

I have my pen, I have my paper
But as for my ideas . . .
None whatsoever.
Writer's block?
So I decide to just write.
Letters make words, make sentences,
Make paragraphs.
Alternatively, letters make words, make lines,
Make verses . . .
Make poetry?
What makes poetry?
Is it the complexity of structure
Or maybe the simplicity?
The rhyming of words?
Maybe it's neither of these.
Is it because it is not a story, a song
A written piece of prose?
Is it a miscellaneous category for when nobody knows
What to call your letter that have
Made words, made lines, made verses

Or is it paragraphs?

Mia-Sara Crowther-Nicol (17)

Fools Fall In Love

The first time I saw you, I was hypnotised
by your piercing blue eyes, you made me
laugh, you made me feel beautiful, our first kiss
was something, I miss, I wish that moment
would last and last

I never thought love was true until I
found you, I only ever believed that fools fall in love
maybe I'm that fool now
I get that butterflies in my stomach kinda feeling
it's magical
woah, woah, woah
you got that look in your eyes
when you smile at me, woahh, I think I love you

You're there to catch me when I fall, you're my best friend
I hope our love will never end
you wipe away my tears and never fail to make me happy
I can see what these love songs are all about

I never thought this would happen to me
meeting you has made me act the way I wanna be
we could be together and know it's for real.

Rebecca Wilson (15)

We Could Have Been

I don't know where to go
I don't know what to do with myself
You're always on my mind
Every day and night
I wonder if you feel the same
The same way that I do

Pre Chorus
I just can't stop thinkin'
About you and I

Chorus
We could have been anything
We could have been everything
We could have been all you wanted
And everything and more

I don't know how it went
I don't know how it ended this way
I think you should know
That for everything I'm sorry
Will you please forgive me or
Can't we just start over?

Stephen Hamilton (16)

La Chica De Mis Suenos (The Girl In My Dreams)

I close my eyes and there she is
Playing on my mind
It's a surprise, it really is
That she is all I find.

She's beautiful, kind and gentle
She can be real sweet
She's beautiful, but kinda mental
That girl I'd like to meet.

Closing my eyes so she's still with me
Standing by my side
She's right there in each of my dreams
She never tries to hide.

She's beautiful, kind and gentle
She can be real sweet
She's beautiful, but kinda mental
That girl I'd like to meet
Never lets me miss a beat
Not that girl I'd like to meet.

Madeline Wilding (16)

You're The One

The first time I saw you I believed you were the one
The one I wanted to be with forever and ever
You gave me a feeling I've never felt before
A feeling I've never experienced
And then I realised I was in love
You make me feel like I'm on top of the world
The happiest girl that there could ever be
When you look in my eyes and tell me how much you love me
I never knew that this much love was real
And the way you make me feel
Baby, I know that you're the one
I love the feeling when we kiss and the softness of your lips
You make me feel like I am an angel
My knight in shining armour you are, my amazing superstar
You make me feel like I'm on top of the world
The happiest girl that there could ever be
When you look in my eyes and tell me how much you love me
I never knew that this much love was real
And the way you make me feel
Baby, I know that you're the one
Yes baby, I know that you're the one.

Cody Frowen (14)

To Say

Nobody knows
Who I am
I want to shine
But I just can't
I wait for someone to come along
To say, 'You are the one, you are the one.'
I just can't wait
For this moment
To see everything so right
I'm waiting for someone, waiting for someone
To say, 'You are the one.'
I'm feeling alone
I don't know why
Just sitting there
Waiting to cry
I look for the moment to shine
I just can't wait, just can't wait
For this moment
To see everything so right
I'm waiting for someone, waiting for someone
To say, 'You are the one.'

Aimee May Walker (13)

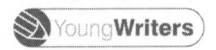

Untitled

She sleeps
Her sculpture of ivy intricately wound around her bodice
Once decorated by the baubles of roses and taffeta lace
Now blackened with the sombre decay of the past
Once upon a time, she made angels cry out in jealousy with her cathedral train
Her sweetheart neckline was one to trace and one to adore
Her gentle ivory colour illuminated by the glow of the sun
Casting rare glimpses of beauty
The trees would whisper her secret, taunting the hearts of the many who remember her
Her empire waistline emphasised by a magical array of pearls and love
Her once worn petticoat lay in the warm mahogany arms of her rocking chair
Her silhouette dances and plays in her shadows
Her almost tapestry-like patters of hearts and dust amalgamate along her gown
Her veil once concealing a face of pureness and gracious hate
Lips like buttons sown together
Eyes like cages, the memories shy away from the bars that obtain them
She awaits for her prince to come and awaken her
From what appears to be
Her final sleep.

Lucy Robson (13)

Rapper's Dream

'Av never been the out loud, outspoken type
Always in deep thought about my life
Like
What am I gonna do when I reach 23?
Be jobless at home, scrapin' together enough money
To get me through the week
Or be on the front page of every magazine
Workin' hard for this rapper's dream?
Thinkin' I could be on TV
Then people tellin' me to get back to reality
Everyone's always doubting me
Though as hard as it seems
I will succeed
In pursuin' this rapper's dream
Have been tested a few times throughout my life
Been offered bad things, always ended up doing right.
I've suffered the pain of loss and cried at night
And have been pushed over the edge, an' had fights
Teeth gritted and my fists clenched tight
I've been though all this an' I'll be all right
As long as my rapper's dream is still in sight.

George Styers (13)

Scream And Shout

Feel the pain
Take the blame
You've lost me
Once again
Taste the tears
Feel the fear
Can't you see
See so clear

There's no going back
You've fallen off track
Cannot turn around
You've hit the ground

Let the hurt out
Scream and shout
Please just stay
No, wait, go away
We're here, we're there
We're everywhere
Finish the fight
Turn out the light.

Caroline Inker (16)

Train Without A Track

Like a train without a track
But in the end we won't come back
Like a boxer with no attack
In the end I just hold back
Maybe I should just go
Stay laid low
And never show
All tucked up beneath the snow
Life's not easy but it's not hard
Stay true and be on your guard
When your time's come you will know
Sometimes it's best to let go
Maybe I should just go
Stay laid low
And never show
All tucked up beneath the snow
Life's a job you cannot fail
Live it good and leave a trail
Uncover your face from beneath that veil
And go and find your holy grail.

Conor McLean (14)

Private School

'Yep, I go to a private school mate'
Man, oh man
That's my 'street rep' down the pan
But what I can never seem to understand
Is why I lose respect due to my intellect
It's winding me up, and getting me vexed
It's like everyone else has come to expect
Me to drink with my pinky erect
But don't worry lads, I'm not gonna defect
To shun this life would be an opportunity wrecked
Because you see
All this money spent gives me the tools that I need
To pave my way to success and in my life succeed
All it takes is a lil' hard work, and determination indeed
And to listen to the words of my teachers
And upon them take heed
Now listen to my voice and hear my creed
Anything can be yours, if you only believe
No matter what school, any goal, any deed
Is yours for the taking if you work for it and seize.

Sam Jellard (15)

In My Heart You'll Always Be

I imagine you looking down at me
From the bright blue sky
Things I want to know
But could you tell me why?

I miss your smile
And seeing your face
Your eyes light up that empty space

In my heart you'll always be
Together we are for eternity

You're a star in the sky at night
Shining so very bright

Tears began to fall from my eyes
Like rain from the dull cloudy skies

We will meet again one day
And all that's left to say

Is I love you so
And will never let you go.

Hannah Sabin (18)

Loving You

I'm not the kind of girl to be taken as a fool
But when I'm in my own world
All I think about is you
You lift me up to heights a bird can't reach
You give me strength to believe in who I am
You catch me when I fall
All I have to do is call and you're there
Do you know how I feel when you're so close to me?
I start to shiver from my head to my feet
I have to walk away before I start to scream
Maybe one day I'll show you how I feel
You lift me up to heights a bird can't reach
You give me strength to believe in who I am
You catch me when I fall
All I have to do is call and you're there
Come and take me, take me away
I love you and I hope you feel the same
I've had enough of dreaming about us two
I just want to be with you.

Emma Louise Carter (13)

Can't Change A Person

Where there's a will there's a way
Can't change what happened yesterday
That day is gone now
Can't change the things you can't see
Can't change the person inside of me

Can't change a person that you've just met
Can't change the things you haven't said
It's too late now and I'll tell you this somehow
Can't change a person, *yeah!*

Georgia May Cresswell (10)

Nothing To Lose

When a moment goes too high
When it falls into the sky
When you smile a beaming smile
When you hold your breath for awhile
When a tear falls down your face
When you feel you've lost the race
When the timer starts to tick
When you know life's gone too quick
When your heart skips a beat
When you know you're in defeat
When it hits you, then you stop
When you realise what you've got
Nothing, almost nothing to lose
You're confused
Not amused
Feel abused
Have to choose
Can't refuse
With nothing, almost nothing to lose.

Catherine O'Neill (14)

Alive

You're in my head,
You're in my heart,
Even when we're apart.
I think about you every day,
I don't know what to say.
Then when I try to speak,
You make my knees go weak.

Chorus
You look at me and I'm lost in your eyes
Then you smile and the stars fill the skies,
You drive me crazy, you don't realise
You make me feel so alive.

Millie Clarke (16)

Reggie

My name is Reggie and I am 65
Although I have been told I look 25
I am in with the gangs pouncing down the street
With my flashing bling and my diamond ring
As I walk down the street I hear people whistling at me
Trying to cuddle me and sometimes even strangle me
But they all love me with my designer hats and my cool raps
What can I say, people love me
And I think I look good with my flashing teeth
It attracts the ladies and they beg at my feet
But I think that I am about to change my look
And go for the more sexier look
Dying my hair black and spraying my teeth white
So when people look at me they see my flashing white teeth
Although I take pride sometimes it can be a bit hard
All this photography and people looking at me
I think I might just go back to being what I was
And then people won't look at me
But at least I will be glad because I am free.

Leanne Drain (15)

Symphonic Romance

The beat reaches every step I find,
Let the music fill the thoughts in my mind,
Carrying me ever near,
To the infinity I've wanted so dear,
The drums create a whirlwind sound,
Pacing through the steady ground,
The cymbals fill my mind and ears,
Devouring all of my fears,
The synth sets a steady flow,
I feel the rhythm through my feet below,
And as the bass begins to start,
The music sets itself in my heart,
As the uncontrollable need to dance,
Sends me into an electronic trance,
Spending my entire life like this,
Is an opportunity I'd never miss,
As my feet continue to dance,
I fall deeper into my,
Symphonic romance.

Yasmin Anderson (14)

Girl Come Back

I want to let you know how much I am missing you
Let my feelings of love be expressed on this tune
The day you left it was so hard to take
Hide my feelings away, put it down to mistakes
Slow dance, romance and kisses through the night
But I guess I wasn't right, making you feel hurt inside
Hindsight shows I really didn't even try
I don't want to move on, I don't want to be gone
I don't want to be that man who says I wish I held on
Your beauty's so hypnotising, there's no way I'd be lying
Rather never love again than know we didn't try it
Still remember the days when you would come out and play
We would be sitting in the sun and soaking up the rays
That's why I want to go back to when we were a fact
If I just got one more chance, I'd swear I'd take that
Regret the things that I did, still had the mind of a kid
But now my mind has grown up and you I want to be with
I'm not just saying this stuff, I know that you've had enough
But I'm going to let go, you're a piece of my soul.

Aaron McBride (18)

Are Men Really Worth It?

Is it worth the ironing?
Is it worth the sweat?
Is it meeting men that you regret?
Is it worth the football?
Is it worth the laze?
Is it worth the betting?
Aww, it drives me to daze.
Is it worth the gas?
Is it worth the fuel?
Is it worth the hot water?
Only if he pays the bill!
Is it worth the tidying?
Is it worth the smell?
Is it worth the Hoovering?
It makes me feel unwell.
So boys are clearly unworthy
Of our feminine charms.
We are not slaves to the opposite gender.
So they can have their own calendar.

Billie-Jean Bradley (12)

Why?

You said goodbye
Just walked away
You made me cry
No words could I say
The dreams that we had
Just never came true
Why did you go
Did you find someone new?
What was it so
We drifted apart?
Why must I live with a broken heart?
If you're filled with regret
But too proud to admit
May my love guide you back
To me here as I sit
Then happy I'd be
No more would I cry
No more to doubt
Or ever ask why?

Jessica White (13)

Fire

Fire, fire burning, burning in my soul
Fire, fire burning in my brain
Fire, fire everywhere but not a bit to burn
You set my soul alight
You make my fire bright
Seconds, seconds after time fades away
Fire, fire burning, going away
Seconds, seconds later time's going slow
Now the fire's going low, low, low
You set my soul alight
You make my fire bright
Water, water coming near
It's a time to fear
Seconds, seconds later
The fire's going out
Not a sound nor a word
It's a time to scream
You put my soul out
You put my fire out.

Louis Metcalf Salerno (11)

A Good Old Life

It was like you were a star
Falling from the sky
Lost in its way
But then you found her
And the light switched back on
And you started gliding again
She must have done something to change you
You were so nice
But what happened?
You changed
The light went back out
The people around you were shocked
You were such a nice lad
So why did you start to rot?
You started to turn back to the old life
Of drugs and booze and drugs
But then you had a close encounter with *death*
You changed your mind and had a good life
You were married and had loads of pie!

Katy Ingoldsby (14)

Icebreaker

My eyes tell it all, looks that once made you shiver . . .
Shared faith in love, I was a believer,
Yes, I dedicated a verse
Word you echoed filled up chapters,
I loved and am not no waiter so am not feeding you on starters,
Am digging your digits 079 me! So we can advance faster,
But racing without no gears, brings out negative energy,
So chasing you only leaves me cardiac arresting, searching,
Can't get over the looks that got me hooked,
What goes on in my mind is what got me shook,
It's all ignorance when I don't approach flybirds,
To me all birds of the same feathers,
All gather in flocks, count me out for that chick,
It is the ego I bring because my palms are cold, so I don't take pics,
Cold-hearted because you're my interest but I only offer kicks . . .
Educated so I put the degree before the chicks,
So I'll be showing them 'what's what',
Widening my horizons so the ice can be worn
But am not looking to finger freeze that.

Philip Bosah (17)

What Are You Doing?

And what may I ask were you doing?
You stood in the rain with me
We lay on the floor laughing
Our bare feet and wiggling toes
We laugh at our past mistakes and chuckle at the future ones
We hold joy in the palm of our hands and with a wand and smiles
We disperse it in the form of one glistening orb
You grimace as it touches your tongue
My slimmer shadow
My little sparrow
We link arms and gossip as we walk
We hold hands and skip
We lay on a hill, we watch the sky and pretend to fly
We wear the rainbow and fill our eyes with clouds
We are best friends
We are so different
And it begs the question
What may I ask are you doing?

Alexandra Dunn (16)

Broken Reflection

All I see here is a broken-hearted girl
She's been waiting for someone to take the pain that's inside her
She may be one of the most beautiful
But when you look deep into her eyes
You can see the tears waiting to come out
He said he loved her, he said he would never leave
But he left her crying on the kitchen floor
Wondering why she just didn't settle for the nerdy boy
Cos even he don't want her now!

Thabile Mdhluli (12)

Incense Narcotics

Sniff, breathe out.
Pot pourri and ash cause havoc with the mind.
Cannabis leaves and druggy's favourite scent
Incenses of rare Tabasco from the East,
Powdered Gold and similies of patchouli and sweated oils.
We see the fluttered spirits of powdered sedatives
And tail the wispy lines of smoke,
Born like a phoenix from the debris on the holder.
Sniff, breathe in.
This time the narcotics of the night play games.
As the candle wax melts the hours away, the scent
Comforts the drunken sleeper. The gold leaf and the
Bellowed smoke dance with each other and tag along
The ceiling. The small flicker of light comes from the
Incense, the dotted light in the clammy night. Protector
Keep me in the incenses' keep, and plaster me with scent
Until morning revival.
Quick, breathe out, before you ruin your senses.

Scott Wilson (16)

Untitled

Loving you is too easy
You're like a breath of fresh air
I've had my heart broken so many times
But you're different
You're perfect in every way
Your hair, your eyes, just everything about you
I would love you more than anything
If only you could see that
The only person I can think about is you
I'll love you always and forever.

Amy Taggart (14)

You Broke My Heart

The other day
I met a boy
Fell in love under the sun
It felt like yesterday
When you walked through the door
My heart melted to the floor
It's nice to know you were there
You'll always be here with your care
Our love has grown apart
Nothing is working
You broke my heart
You were the one I adored
Now I want you even more
You broke my heart
Every time I see your face
It makes me feel a state
Don't know just how you did it
But it worked real good.

Danielle Clarke (11)

My Dreamgirl

Follow me and I'll take you on a journey
Through the world and absolute eternity
Oh my God, my heart rate has just raised
Every time I look at you I'm quite amazed
From the past, to the present, to the future
I'll treat you right, not like a piece of furniture
You're the world, you're the sun, you're the sky
Between you and me, there's no lie
You send my head into a whirl
You to me will always be a dreamgirl.

Tariq Bushara (13)

Fertile Fields

These tranquil times bring hollow lines
And as the paint drips from your eyes
The sum of your fears
These lonely tears
Can pull your fingers from your ears
For you must bleed, your tongue to feed
And backwards rhymes won't do

And as you scream in the fertile fields
Your throat cracks with fruits of virtue
Your cries drown in a tortured whisper of truth

Dancing on graves with no one in
As green grass grows untouched
In fertile fields
Looking for pain won't heal
Painting the thorns when the rose is real
Scream at the sky for being blue
Your drowning cries are coming true.

Ali Mansfield (15)

Mulberry Lane

And this burst of memories
Was spurred on by
The fact that I had changed
I wish I could go back and take the years
To have them all rearranged

In my head
I am taking a train
That stops every day
On Mulberry Lane.

Kelsey Griffin (15)

The Space In-Between

The shapes are my world
They define my being
Moving, shifting, changing form
Sometimes near, occasionally fleeing.

But when they have gone
I am left with nothing
Just the space in-between.

When I am alone and the tears run free
Then I can't work out the meaning
Of the shapes around me

And all I can reach
Is the space in-between.

It is a place to hide
Where you cannot be seen
It is numbness, escape
It is the space in-between.

Amy Clark (14)

Best Day Of My Life

You thought I knew what it meant, when I first met you.
'Cause now I'm left all alone with nothing left to say or do.
But one day I'm sure it will come right back together,
Without you I'm nothing at all.
Then baby when I saw you it all changed because . . .
It was the best day of my life,
It was the best day of my life.
I thought I had lost you but now it's all come true
'Cause there was me and you.

Cath Nobbs (10)

Torn

I know at times it's hard
To see sense through all the confusion
To understand the reason why
To smile through your desertion

The ones you love, on whom you depend
Never stay around long
Every time they walk away
You know that you were wrong

Wrong to trust and wrong to hope
For them to always care
Wrong to smile and wrong to love
For life just isn't fair

There seems no end, no reprieve
From this torturous pain
So why is it we all insist
To smile and start again?

Charlotte Hilsdon (17)

Love Lost, Never To Be Found

We were meant to be together, but now it's goodbye.
I'm going insane just looking for lyrics that described,
where we had gone wrong.
Wishing you would show me love for one last time.
Knowing we will never be together, again!
The pain is hard to bare but I have to carry on.
The fun times were shared are just a glimmer of hope.
The good times are remembered, the bad are lost.
Moving on from you is a nightmare which cannot be stopped.
Hoping both of us will find love once again.
We were meant to be together,
but now it's goodbye forever, to the end!
That which is lost shall never be found.

Stephanie Henry (16)

The End

Every breath I take
My life comes closer to its end,
My heart slowly but surely starts to slow
And my body, one day will take a blow.

My inner spirit will somehow rise
And take its place in Heaven,
Leaving behind a pale, motionless body, a cage of free thoughts,
Just a trace of what I used to be.

I hope to return to my former reality,
As a being of debatable existence,
Just to check up on everyone and everything,
Even if it's only for a minute.

I don't know why I'm afraid of dying,
Because I hope for a peaceful end,
But I will try to never forget,
That the end is a new beginning.

Madeline King (13)

Your Face

The stars are your eyes
The sun is your mouth
The trees are your hair
And the world
Is your face.

It's in the stones
Of ruined Saint's Church
It's in the water
Of the Thames
It's in the words
Of this song.

It's in my heart
It's your face.

Amy Wooding (16)

Love And Hope

I can wait if it means we'll be together one day
You're leaving this September and I'll see you next May
Just promise you'll be careful, I know you can't stay
But I need to know you'll be okay.

I'll miss you every day, I can't pretend that's not true
You looked me in the eyes and said it's what you need to do
We'll marry, move away, when all of this is through
But in the meantime I'll need you.

When there's a knock at the door or the phone makes a sound
I'll get someone else to answer it if they are around
Put my head in my hands and pray, get down on the ground
Hoping it's not you that they've found.

Until you return I'll sleep on your side of the bed
Always hearing In my mind the last thing that you said,
'Every hour, every day you'll be in my heart and my head,
Treat each day with love and hope, not fear and dread.'

Nina Baldwin (15)

Arriving At Hell's Gate

My life has come to pass
Running down like an hourglass
How much longer will I have to wait
Before arriving at Hell's gate?

This life I have wasted
I don't think I'd wanna live it again
Death's presence I have tasted
Come and get me, I don't want to remain!

Come and get me, I'm sat here watching
Nothing to do, just waiting for you to come
Kill me now like I want you to
At least in Hell I'll have some fun.

Jack Burton (13)

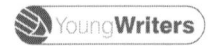

It's Always Me

It's hard being the youngest one
Life isn't always very fun
For everything you get the blame
Till you get so cross it feels insane
It's hard being told you're always wrong
When people have been saying that for so long
I need to prove the fault's not mine
Till then, I'll never feel sublime
I'm always the one to get rebuked
Although I didn't start the dispute
Then I'll try to prove I'm right
Somehow, I'll never win the fight
The argument will always end in tears
Though an hour ago, I was in good cheer
Why did things have to change?
Well, I know inside, I'm not to blame.

Georgina Wong (13)

Dreams

Why do dreams feel real at night?
Why does my heart take flight?
I'm following my dreams for once
I'm making sure I'm following my heart
Not yours
I can be strong without you
I don't love you anymore
But you still love me
I don't want to remember you
Or anything about you
I hate you
You were my best friend
My soulmate
But you're not anymore
So goodbye.

Aaron James Walton (12)

Decimals

Smile for the camera
Your cavalry's arrived
Bright blue eyes for the camera
But the lens is way too wise.

All smiles for the camera
Why should you need to try?
Numbers lend reality
To the truth that underlies.

Prove my point like a decimal
You deal in recurring lies
In maths there's inequalities
In love there's compromise.

Smile for the camera
These seeds here in my hand
Are not chaos but compassion
Full of love and compromise.

Kirsty Keatch (17)

Untitled

When I look in the mirror
All I can see is
The slightly-too-big hips
And the bum jeans never seem to fit
The too many spots across my face
And the skin that's so pale, it looks like paste
I fail to notice
Those deep, dark, sparkling eyes
Or how my hair changes shade in the sunlight
I don't see the pretty face that people tell me I have
Or my individual style that means I can't be classed as emo or chav
When the world is full of criticism and negativity
How you do expect teenage girls to look at themselves positively?

Tarryn Layla Hiller (14)

Dream Untrue

There was two, and now there's one,
It's not the same without you.
I miss your smile, your Armani scent
And the way you took care of me.

You came along, you changed my world.
I'm so sad that it didn't work.
It felt so warm to be with you,
Now it's cold and every teardrop starts to freeze.

You took the only thing that beat in me,
I tried to get you out of my head.
So many memories I try to chase, after you.
But all it is, is a dream untrue.

The way you left, without a word,
No bye-bye, not even an excuse.
Where was the love, that we shared,
How did it disappear without a trace?

Nicole Andrea Gonzalez (12)

We Make The World

People say 'be this'
Magazines shout 'do this,'
I reply, why?
Size zeros, chavs and thugs
Barbie dolls and plain average Joes
So many types of people
Yet, only one you!
You, who diminishes categories of people
Stands up and declares
I am me,
You are you
We are the individuals
Who make the world.

Priyashree K Patel (16)

Waiting

And I know you can't breathe
At the edge of your seat
Holding onto what we have
But baby we'll make it
Because I'm starting to figure out
That I cannot live without you
And that's all we need for now
You're inches from my fingertips
But this is what we've waited so long for
Wouldn't have it any other way
'Cause this is what I've been waiting so long for
I don't want you any other way
I just want you here with me.

Kelly Scutt (16)

Trees In The Forest

The trees sway
They lead the way
Through the forest darkness
You see them there in front of you
Looming, towering, tall
In the morning
I'll have a look
To see if they're still
Swaying at me
Like the day before
Perhaps even more
They follow you everywhere
To see if you even care
They nestle in the wind
They creak and crackle when a storm is due
I laugh at the short and stubby trunks
They're *trees of the forest!*

Stephanie Jane Parker (8)

Friday Night Clubbing

Dancing is my escape
to where I wanna be
When I hit the dance floor
I start to come alive
The DJ turns it up
The people start to jump
I love the sound
of the thumping beat
that makes you jump
off your seat
The music runs
deep inside my veins
The vibes go right to my brain
Bright lights fill the room
that penetrates the deepening gloom
and when the people start to leave
I will still be dancing.

Catriona Mair (13)

Moving On

When I watched you walk out the door,
I needed to go out and tell you,
That I don't want to be with you anymore,
We need to sit down and talk it through.

I really thought our love would last forever,
I guess my dreams were wrong,
But dreams don't come true; hardly ever,
I just think that our love isn't that strong.

So, I guess this is goodbye,
We just have to move on,
You're just not my type of guy,
I'm sorry but our time has gone.

Erin Harvey (12)

My Whole Life

You seek all my care and my attention
You want all my time, right on the line
Oh, oh, oh, oh argh!

All you want is me forever
My only secret is . . .
I really just need the time

I love the whole of my life
The whole of my life
C'mon Baby, c'mon
You and me, me and you
Just you and me for life
Oh, oh, oh.

Daisy Caig (13)

Go, go, go!

Put on ma helmet, get on ma bike
Ah roll, roll, roll on through the night
Go, go, go, go
Put on ma skates
Roll down the path
All the way through
Ah laugh, laugh, laugh
Go, go, go, go

Jump on ma scooter
Fly down the hill
Oh it give me such a thrill
Go, go, go, go

Get off ma scooter
I'm gonna drop
I get in the door and say . . .
Stop, stop, stop!

Leah Knox (12)

Lyrics On My Heart

Your smile's like music to my ears
it fills me with you
as you write lyrics on my heart
I fall in love in your eyes
I can almost see inside
your voice is getting weak

Every soulful chord
every beautiful word
I fall to the ground
as my heart begins to pound
play me music, play me music
as I go to dreamland

You help me climb a tree of confidence
you help me reach my stars
they are my dreams
and they're yours to keep.

Lisa Fairley (16)

Music Rules!

Music keeps me smiling,
Music is the best,
Without the thumping rhythm,
It would not stand out amongst the rest.

Singing, dancing, clapping along.
Always there making a fantastic song.
I'm so glad music is everything,
Makes my life fun, the best . . . so happy.

So if you have not experienced this,
Change your life quick and experience bliss.
Music! Music! shout out loud.
Looking for lyrics, be yourself - don't follow the crowd!

Jessica Cordery Prince (13)

Scared Of Losing You

Please don't leave me, you are the only one I can trust
No one else as faithful as you and your love just doesn't stop
Stayed awake so many nights trying to understand
Why I'm so scared of losing my other half
You were a blessing from up above, never been so damn in love
Never been so scared of losing you, you, you, you
Going through this phase, you are the only thing I can't replace
Irreplaceable to be baby, can't you see
So scared of losing all I've ever wanted
You were the empty spaces for need and praise
Scared of losing you, you, you, you
Scared of losing you, you, you, you
The way you used to say my name was so magical
I just wish I had the courage you did
So scared of losing you, you, you, you
Scared of losing you, you, you, you.

Catriona Cormack (12)

Motivation

This is not what I planned it to be
I thought maybe you could see
How my life has turned around
And that we have touched the ground
Don't have to say it twice
You disgust me little spice
Don't try and run away yet!
This is not what I want
The motivation is killin' me
The way you look at me
I really see somethin'
I don't wanna be.
I don't wanna be.

Jasmine Clarke (10)

Twisted Heart Strings

My heart's twisted as if it's a cinema ticket
In the palm of a grim and harsh critic
I'm still as artistic as I used to be
But these dim and dark visions are using me
I grin and laugh cos when you harness youth you're free
Never swallow my pride, I follow ruthless dreams
Love will never die, it's a gifted art
You're more likely to see Siamese twins drift apart
But more than anything I love your feminine tone
So genuine mind soothing my medicine
Delicate but with the power of an elephant
You could crush any man so effortless
Definite, beauty is what her weapon is
And I'm a junkie, I need a second kiss
It takes the p*** that I depend on this
But you hurt my heart I need to mend a bit.

Harry Sadeghi (19)

If You Don't Listen

If you don't listen, listen
You won't get the grades you need
And you won't get a good education
And you won't get a good education
English, science, geography
Maths, history, art
They all make you smart
You start at primary and some end in uni
And you will get a good education
And you will get a good education
English, science, geography
Maths, history, art
They all make you smart.

Paige Band (12)

Soaring

Flying over what could never be
Longing
Wishing for a life containing just you and me
Hoping
For a way this could all come true
Yet
I know that this is all just stupid to you
I don't wanna explain myself to you
If I did, I know you would never let this come true
So I'll keep it locked away
It'll wait
It'll stay
Longing for one special day.

Lauren Degenhardt (15)

The End Of Love!

I can't believe you said we're history
I thought we had some chemistry
And now you've got no feelings for me
I just want you to leave me be
I never wanted this fantasy to end
Just thinking about it drives me round the bend
When we met you were my whole life, my heart
But now you've torn it apart
You don't know how happy I was with you
Honestly, you don't have a clue
I loved you from the very start
But now you have broken my heart
I have been badly hypnotised
By all your ugly lies
But now you have left me
I just feel so empty!

Megan Roberts (14)

Without You

I can't forget you leaving
Or the way you left me
You made me feel so happy
Not a day was I down
I wonder as the day passes
Why did you leave me?
I wish we could get back together
My heart slows by the minute without you
I wish you were here, stood by me now
I'm so emotional without you
I can't pretend to not love you anymore
When you will always have a place in my heart
What did I do wrong?
I wonder, day in and day out will I get you back?
I never meant to hurt you
And I love you so much still.

Jade Bond (12)

No More Hiding

Close your eyes
Feel the disguise
Hide within and bury your soul
Close the shell and fight the demon
Shut down and feel the cold
Leak a while
Fake a smile
Feel alone and close the door
Quiver and shake
You're scared
You're sore
Can this pain go on much more?
Wake up!
It's your time to shine
Take off that disguise and show your eyes.

Michelle Vincent (18)

Lucy's Rap

My name is Luce
And I like apple juice
I go to school
Cos I'm nobody's fool
I live at Newby West
Where swimming's what I do best
Wednesday is the day I go
Where I swim and swim to and fro
I've got a rabbit named Peter
He's such a good eater
He runs round and round
Covering all the ground
This is my rap, all about me
Hope you've enjoyed it
And it fills you with glee!

Lucy Jane Wilkinson (13)

Would You Care?

Would you care if I was going to die?
Would you even cry?
The reason I'm asking you why,
Is because you sigh every time I talk to you
And you say, 'What now?'
Every time we spend time together
We always seem to row.
I don't really see what the point is right now.
Nobody ever understand why I'm trying to say
And when they actually listen
They take everything the wrong way.
Please give me a hug and tell me
That everything will be OK.
And then my broken heart
Will survive another day.

Claire Harrity (15)

Confident Not Cocky

I'm not an angel, no halo
But I'm not a criminal, no way, so
I won't do time because I've chosen street rhyme
Forget robbery cos I will never do crime
I want to make it big, be the best MC
Won't stop till I drop when I'm seventy
And by then I hope to make millions
And have a legion of fans that say I'm brilliant
You know I'm confident, not cocky
I get better and better like I'm Rocky
The rest are like Primark compared to me, Prada
They think they go hard but I know I go harder
From day dot I've been gifted with lyrics
Never had to use repetitive gimmicks
Still I understand I have to keep feet on ground
If I want to take home the microphone king crown.

David Elliott (15)

Papa Roach Title Song

I'm on a never-ending binge
But really, all I want is to be loved
My behaviour is reckless and I live days of war
Nights of love deceive me with hidden snakes
Seething with revenge, wishing and wanting to take me
I need to stop looking/start seeing
If I ever want to be free from my decompression period
Black clouds absorb all my energy
I'm proof that life is a bullet
Walking through barbed wire is painful
Emerging from a broken home
Must rebuild a tattered legacy
Must march out of the darkness
Must escape, start my metamorphosis.

Caitlin Kitchener (15)

Life's Too Short (For Poverty)

All these people wonderin' why millions of diseases 'bout to multiply
We've got the money, so we should sort it out
There's no time left to pause and think of doubt
There's things in this world we can't live without
We all need some help to get them, we all have to figure it out
What we gonna do to set these people free?
Think about others and not just me
Open up our eyes, the picture's there to see
There's no need in this world for poverty
We gotta understand, we gotta know
The right way to turn these people, the right way to go
Just pray to God and hopefully He'll show
Us the directions, roads, He wants us to take
Give us all His tools, show how He can make
The world into something it was meant to be
It's about high time people looked at the reality
Go to the worst off countries, see what's going' on
It's everyone's fault, ask yourself, where did you go wrong?

Katherine Kennedy (18)

Dad

When you've lost someone close
Like your mum or your dad
You remember all the good times that you both had.
So you sit and you wish that they were still here
But in your sleep and your dreams they always appear.
When you're round people you fake a smile
But when you get home you cry, for a while.
So in reality they're dead and gone
But in your heart and dreams they will always live on.

André White

Magician

He talks sharp, a charmer
He delights the crowd
That's formed around him
He's loud and he's astounding
He's got tricks and talent
He looks for a target he can make
One that can't tell he's just fake
He's a one trick pony
Gets attention only
From his rehearsed act
He does it over and over
He gains appreciation
But it's straight manipulation
I feel sorry for the bunny
That disappears under his hat
Can't distinguish fiction from fact
It's all just an act
No one likes a name-dropper, friend-hopper
'Look at me' type, show-stopper
I won't be blinded.

Anna Goodman-Jones (16)

Looking For Lyrics - The Song In My Heart

Young Writers Information

We hope you have enjoyed reading this book - and that you will continue to enjoy it in the coming years.

If you like reading and writing poetry drop us a line, or give us a call, and we'll send you a free information pack.

Alternatively if you would like to order further copies of this book or any of our other titles, then please give us a call or log onto our website at www.youngwriters.co.uk

Young Writers Information
Remus House
Coltsfoot Drive
Peterborough
PE2 9JX
(01733) 890066